THE LIBRARY
MARY'S COLLEGE OF MARYLAND
MARY'S CITY, MARYLAND 20686

Da Capo Press Music Reprint Series
GENERAL EDITOR:
FREDERICK FREEDMAN
Vassar College

METHOD FOR THE SPANISH GUITAR

Sor's Method

FOR THE

Spanish Guitar,

TRANSLATED FROM THE ORIGINAL

BY

A. MERRICK.

LONDON:

R. COCKS AND CO., 20, PRINCES-STREET, HANOVER-SQUARE.

NEW MUSIC FOR THE SPANISH GUITAR,

PUBLISHED AS ABOVE.

INSTRUCTION BOOKS.	*s.*	*d.*
NUSKE's Method, with Twenty-seven Airs	5	0
CARULLI's Method	4	0
VOICE AND GUITAR.		
PELZER's Fifty National Songs each	0	6
HAGART's Le Papillon, 6 books each	1	6

PIANOFORTE AND GUITAR.	*s.*	*d.*
NÜSKE's Weber's Last Waltz	1	6
——— Beethoven's ditto	1	6
——— Alpine Melody	1	6
——— Souvenir's de l'Opera, 72 Airs, 12 books, each	2	6
FLUTE AND GUITAR.		
LE BOUQUET, Collection of elegant Airs, 6 books, each	1	6

[*W. Fowler, Printer, Cirencester.*]

THE LIBRARY
ST. MARY'S COLLEGE OF MARYLAND
ST. MARY'S CITY, MARYLAND 20686

Method for the Spanish Guitar

By Ferdinand Sor

Translated by A. Merrick

DA CAPO PRESS • NEW YORK • 1971

A Da Capo Press Reprint Edition

This Da Capo Press edition of
Method for the Spanish Guitar
is an unabridged republication of the
first edition published in London.

Library of Congress Catalog Card Number 77-158960
SBN 306-70188-X

Published by Da Capo Press, Inc.
A Subsidiary of Plenum Publishing Corporation
227 West 17th Street, New York, N.Y. 10011
All Rights Reserved

Manufactured in the United States of America

METHOD FOR THE SPANISH GUITAR

METHOD

FOR

THE SPANISH GUITAR,

BY

Ferdinand Sor.

TRANSLATED FROM THE ORIGINAL

BY

A. MERRICK.

London:

R. COCKS & Co., 20, PRINCES-STREET, HANOVER-SQUARE.

CIRENCESTER: PRINTED BY WILLIAM FOWLER.

CONTENTS.

ERRATA.

Page 9, line 1, after strings, add ; and *but*.
— 23, line 12, for *XXXI.* read *XXX.*
— 29, line 3, for *XVI.* read *XVII.*
— 36, last line, for *XV.* read *XIV.*

SOR'S METHOD FOR THE GUITAR.

INTRODUCTION.

In writing a method, I would be understood to speak of that only which my reflections and experience have made me establish to regulate my own play. If certain precepts are in contradiction to the practice heretofore adopted by guitarists who, through blind submission, and a religious respect for their masters, have followed their maxims without examining the foundation of them, it would be wrong to suppose in me a spirit of opposition. I have exalted no maxim into a principle, till after a due consideration of the motives for so doing; I establish nothing by authority nor by caprice; and I merely indicate the route which I have followed in order to produce results from the guitar which have obtained for me the approbation of harmonists, people the most difficult to satisfy and to dazzle in regard to music. I do not believe that my compositions for this instrument can be executed on different principles; I write therefore only for those who, believing the execution to be almost unattainable, have the goodness to consider me as a phenomenon, whilst I possess no greater means than another person. Music, reasoning, and the preference which I give in general to results before a display of difficulty, constitute my whole secret. Their astonishment arises only from the manner in which they consider the guitar: while they say that this instrument is principally intended for accompaniment, classing it therefore among the instruments of harmony, they always begin by treating it as an instrument of melody; for their first lessons are always scales, to which they accustom the fingering. This fingering habituating them from the first to employ all the powers of the left hand for the melody, causes them to experience great difficulties when it becomes requisite to add a correct base, unless it be afforded by the open strings (*a*), and still much greater difficulties when one or two intermediate parts are to be added besides. For them the fingering in this case is only a continual deviation from the rules which habit has established as a law; and to this let us add the inconveniency of finding themselves without the least support for the guitar, because being obliged to place the whole hand on the strings to make a chord, they cannot of course leave one half behind the neck, as they do for supporting it. It is therefore quite natural that, by extending results to which not only their fingering has no tendency, but from which it misleads them, I am gratified with the title of extraordinary; and that persons, who have never heard me, say it is impossible that I can play all that I write; but in reality I am far from being a wonder. I love music, I feel it: the study of harmony and counterpoint having familiarized me with the progression and nature of chords and their inversions, with the manner of throwing the melody or air into the base or into one of the intermediate parts, of increasing the number of notes of one or two parts, whilst the others continue their slower progression, I have required things of this kind from the instrument, and I have found that it yields them better than a continual jumble of semi and demisemi-quavers, in diatonic and chromatic scales.

At first I took up this instrument merely as an instrument of accompaniment; but, from the age of sixteen years, I was shocked to hear it said by those who professed to have but little talent, "I only play to accompany". I knew that a good accompaniment supposes in the first place a good base, chords adapted to it, and movements as much as possible approximating those of an orchestral score or those of a pianoforte; things which, in my opinion, afforded a much greater proof of mastery on the instrument than all those sonatas which I heard with long violin

(*a*) Some have thought to remedy this inconvenience by adding a number of covered strings to the guitar; but, would it not be simpler to learn to employ the six — Add resources to an instrument when you have drawn every possible advantage from those which it offers; but do not attribute to the instrument what you should impute to yourselves.

passages, without harmony or even devoid of base, excepting the base found on the open strings. Hence I concluded that there were no masters for me, and I was confirmed in the idea that what was taken for mastery on the instrument was the very cause preventing its attainment (*b*). By dint of playing accompaniment, I found myself in possession of a stock of positions; and as I knew what chord or what inversion I played, its contexture and derivation (*c*), in what part the fundamental base was found, and what ought to be the progression of every part for the resolution or transition about to be made, I found myself prepared to establish a complete system of harmony on this instrument: this system was, it might be said, telegraphic; for every position of my four fingers representing a chord, I found myself in a situation to see a figured base, and, without taking up the guitar, to indicate the harmonic progression by the configurations alone.

In accompanying airs of Italian operas, I frequently met with little melodious passages in some instrumental part, and by endeavouring to execute them on the guitar, I found that the fingering which I employed for harmony was the basis of that which I found necessary for the melody, and that the latter should be almost entirely dependant on the former. Success having completely crowned my wishes, I wrote a few pieces, with little consideration I admit, which, however prepared the route that circumstances obliged me to follow, and which I have only had to examine severely in order to correct my manner of writing since I have become a professor. Several of these pieces would have never been exposed to the public, had I been consulted; but some persons who had copies (most of them incorrect) communicated them to the editor, who, doing far to much honour to my talents, seized with pleasure every thing that bore my name. However, since they are published, they may serve to prove how many useful reflections I have made since, if compared with my twenty-four lessons and my twenty-four studies: these reflections I am now about to communicate and explain to the reader. By examining them, he will be able to judge whether they are as useful as I think them, or whether I am blind on the subject. Far from pretending to affect a modesty which might appear liable to suspicion, I confess having been recently convinced by experience that he who should tell me that *there are some things which how just soever they may appear in theory, are not so by any means in practice* would find this observation disproved by Miss Wainwright, a young English Lady, whose accurate reasoning, readiness of apprehension, the conviction that my precepts were the only ones that could enable her to obtain from the guitar the desired effects, and the little application that her other studies and the claims of society allowed her, produced a result so flattering to me, that in twenty-five lessons she played perfectly the six little pieces that I have dedicated to her, and understood all my twenty-four lessons so well as no longer to require any person to enable her to discover the best fingering of all imaginable positions: her figure and her hands are so placed as to serve as a model. It is true that she likes to find reasons for everything she does, and that I have never had a pupil possessing so good a way of studying nor so analytical a mind.

Without doubt I shall be told that the reasons which I give for having established my precepts require for their comprehension other knowledge than that of music, and that the present work is unsuited to an amateur whose object is not the deep study of an instrument which, according to general opinion, requires a great deal of time and labour. That remark may appear at first view to be just; but on reflection it will be found of no force. An amateur is he who takes up the study of the instrument as a relaxation from his serious occupations. He has therefore learnt other things, he must have reasoned; his education has initiated him in the elements of the sciences of which the knowledge was indispensable to him; he should love reason and prefer it to authority; he ought therefore to comprehend me better than he who has employed his whole time in studying music. As to professors, I do not pretend to give them lessons; and those who may not be able to comprehend me will never say so; for the Royal Library having its doors open, and the Encyclopedia being at the command of any who wish to consult it, even if my work did not deserve the trouble, they would always take a step interesting to their self-love and from which they would derive real advantage for the future.

(*b*) At that time I had not heard of Mr. Frederic Moretti. I heard one of his accompaniments performed by a friend of his, and the progression of the base, as well as the parts of the harmony which I distinguished, gave me a high idea of his merit. I considered him as the flambeau which was to serve to illuminate the wandering steps of guitarists.

(*c*) The derivatives signify quite the contrary to that which I mean to say here.

It may be useful to some readers to remark, that a chord is a combination of musical sounds differing in pitch, according to the rules of harmony; that one letter, or note, in every chord is called its root, or fundamental sound; and that when the root is the base, or lowest sound, the chord is said to be direct, but when any other of its letters is made the base, the chord is said to be inverted: thus a chord formed of four letters may have three inversions. Inversions are sometimes called derivatives.—Tr.

PART I.

THE INSTRUMENT.

As I shall never say to the reader—*This is what is necessary to be done*, but *this is what I found necessary to do*, so neither shall I say how a guitar ought to be made, but how it should be made for me, and for what reasons.

In order that the belly or sounding-board may be set in vibration sufficiently by the impulse communicated by the vibrating string, it should be made thin and of very light wood. But being as thin as necessary for the prolongation of the sound, the strong and continual tension of the bridge would compel it to give way in a little while, and it would be pressed inwards. To prevent its giving way, the manufacturers have contrived ribs or bars inside. If these ribs are strong enough to support the force of the bridge (equal to the united tension of all the strings, plus the impulse received from the fingers of the right hand) they must necessarily hinder a great part of the vibrations of the sounding board; and if they are weak enough to enter into vibration themselves, they will not prevent the sounding board

Fig. 1.

Fig. 2.

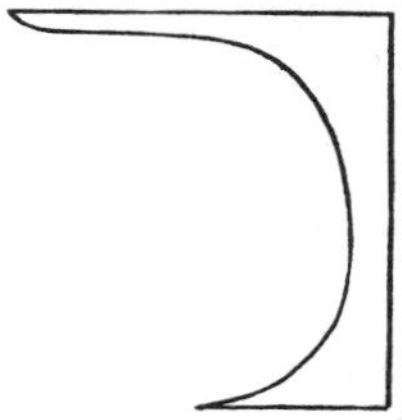

from giving way eventually. I think I can shew that a bridge of the form represented by fig. 1, constructed of a single piece, and an inside bracket, made as seen in profile by perpendicular section in fig. 2, would answer the object desired. Experiment has proved it in London, where Mr. J. Panormo made some guitars under my direction, as well as Mr. Schroeder at Petersburgh. But these facts do not allow me to dispense with the demonstration.

Fig. 3.

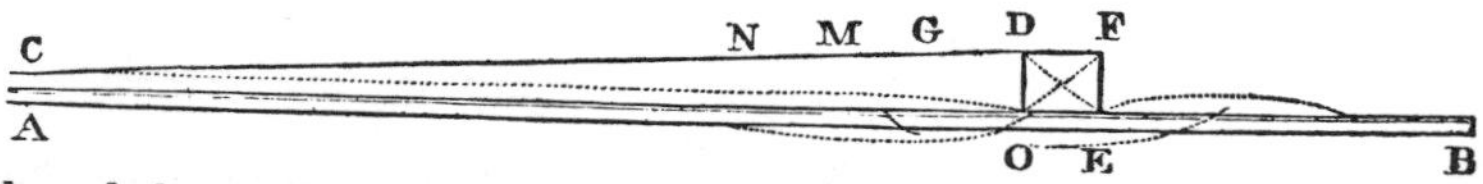

If on a sounding board the profile of which is represented by the line A B, fig. 3. the bridge D O E F be fixed, the tension of the string, C D will cause the point D to have a strong and continual tendency towards the point G, and this point towards the point M, which in its turn will have the same towards N, and so on; for the constant action of the head containing the pegs is to draw towards it whatever forms an obstacle to hold the other end of the strings from approaching it. To resist this great combination of tensions, there is only the short arm of the lever D E, because, as long as the bridge holds its place, D may be considered as a fulcrum. It is very easy to see that the power and the resistance are in the arms of their respective levers, and that the point D is much more drawn towards C, than towards F. He who would dissent from this conclusion would think it disproved by observing to me that the adhesion of the bridge to the sounding-board by means of glue, and sometimes even by screws, is much more powerful than the tension of the strings; but this objection would complete my demonstration. I have never observed that the solidity with which the bridge is fixed to the sounding-board so far exceeded the force of tension of the strings as to cause them all to break, and I have often seen the strings pull off the bridge, an accident which I can speak of from experience at my own expense, for my right hand suffered from it for several days. But even supposing that might never happen, and that the two powers were in the inverse ratio of the arms of their levers, it is not the less true that in the obtuse angle C D E, the point D, which is impelled by two very powerful agents towards the point O, will bear upon it with the sum of the forces C D + D E, and that these two lines tending to become one line only, C E, with a force and tenacity which the sounding-board would not long resist, it must give way at the point O. As soon as the point E, becomes raised, it either separates, or rather, tending to raise up the part E B, eventually cracks the sounding-board.*

Fig. 4,

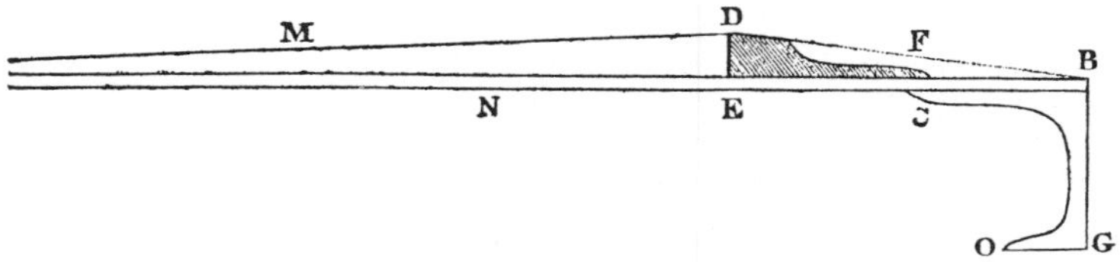

The prolongation of the bridge D, E, F, fig. 4. coinciding with that of the bracket C, B, G, O, produces a line of support E, B, much longer than the distance O, E, fig. 3. so that the line D, B, may be considered as the direction of resistance. The angle M, D, B, being more obtuse, ought to cause less pressure to become a straight line to which it more nearly approximates. The point F, being more distant from the point E, besides comprising more glued surface, cannot occasion the part F B, of the sounding board to rise, being identified with the prolongation of the upper part of the bracket C B; and the part N E, having no resistance to oppose, may be as thin as will be suitable to the quality and continuation of the tone.

With me, the most essential point has always been the form the direction and the placing of the neck. I have always preferred a guitar with little tone and the neck placed as I require it, to a guitar with a full tone and the neck placed differently; because in the first case I can produce as much tone as it is capable of yielding, and in the second case I can produce only half, excepting with the open strings.

Fig. 5.

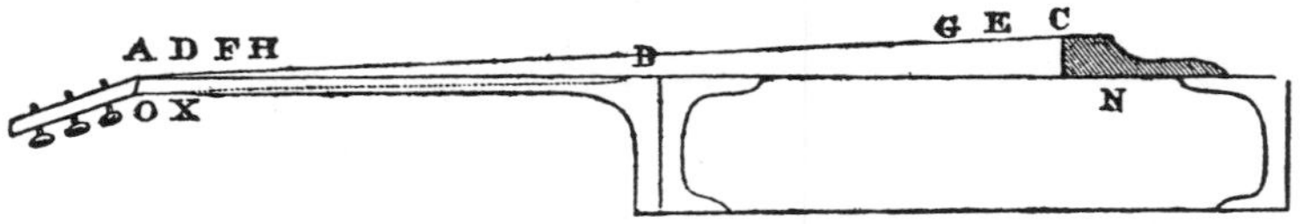

The string A C, fig. 5. is incontestably more flexible at the point B, than at the points D, E, F, G, &c. Now, in order that the finger which is to press it on the points D, F, H, &c. should experience the same resistance, it is necessary that the distance between the string and the finger-board should increase in the direct ratio of the flexibility. I therefore require that the height of the nut shall have the same relation with the height of the first fret, as the latter has with the second fret; for, in proportion as the frets approach the lower end of the finger-board, they should progressively diminish. By this means I find the same resistance everywhere, and consequently the same

* I shall not meddle with this "demonstration", further than to observe, that it chiefly concerns the manufacturer; and that an instrument-maker, to profit by his experience, should be an accurate mechanical draughtsman, understand the common principles of mechanics, the composition and resolution of forces, and the laws of vibrating strings and surfaces; but these subjects may be dispensed with by the mere performer, and are useful to him only in guiding his judgement of instruments.—Tr.

facility in pressing the strings as the covered or spun strings, in proportion as they increase in depth of sound, are more rarely employed in very quick passages, the line of the bridge on which they bear must not be quite parallel to the plane of the sounding-board, but a little more elevated on the side of the sixth string. This elevation does not occasion any very considerable difference for the left hand; but it is very advantageous for the right hand, allowing me readily to produce stronger and more lengthened bases when required. The bridge if too low prevents my touching the strings properly, as I shall shew when I come to that article: the bridge too high, removing the string too far from the direction parallel to the sounding-board, the sound would lose much of its strength and especially of its roundness. That the bridge may be of the proper height without removing the strings too far from the finger-board, I have the line N, O, divided into two parts, B, N, and B, A, and from the point B, it takes a direction towards the point X. This deviation, besides greatly facilitating the play of the left hand, has a considerable influence on the tone of the instrument. The proofs of my assertion would give me the air of wishing to instruct the guitar-makers, and it might be justly remarked that I was wandering from the object of the present work. Besides, they ought to know in what the quantity and quality of the tone of the instrument consists, and by what means the component parts contribute to them. The curve forming the convexity of the fingerboard must not exceed an arc of 18 degrees, and should at its extremities take very slightly the form of a semi-ellipsis. The part on which the frets are fixed should be a plane surface, for the reasons which I shall give when I come to speak of the left hand. The head containing the pegs should neither be in a straight line with the finger-board, nor inclined backward so far as to form an angle greater or less than from 24 to 26 degrees. For the rest, having no relation with my subject, I should not speak of it, more especially as the manner of constructing the body of the instrument is almost everywhere understood extremely well, and most Neapolitan, German, and French guitars leave in this respect very little superiority to the Spanish. In the goodness of the body or box, the Neapolitan guitars in general long surpassed, in my opinion, those of France and Germany; but that is not the case at present, and if I wanted an instrument, I would procure it from M. Joseph Martinez of Malaga, or from M. Lacote, a French maker, the only person who, besides his talents, has proved to me that he possesses the quality of not being inflexible to reasoning. This skilful artist is very frequently obliged to satisfy those who consider the instrument otherwise than I do, and makes guitars on which it is impossible to play my music or any other that has the base and other parts of the harmony always proceeding correctly; but let a good instrument be ordered of him, leaving him at liberty to make it as he pleases, he will make one for me, and he who on trying it might find it defective, should attribute the cause to his way of employing it.

The guitars to which I have always given the preference are those of Alonzo of Madrid, Pagès and Benediz of Cadiz, Joseph and Manuel Martinez of Malaga, or Rada, successor and scholar of the latter, and those of M. Lacote of Paris. I do not say that others do not exist; but never having tried them, I cannot decide on that of which I have no knowledge. I ought to repeat that the faults which I have found in several guitars, I have not always attributed to the ignorance nor the obstinacy of the makers. These defects are frequently required by the guitarists, who, instead of blaming their own way of touching the strings, blame the instrument, and would have it accommodate itself to their play, instead of accommodating themselves to its nature. For my own part, when I have heard a string jar, I have examined first whether the fault proceeded from the bad conformation of the instrument or from my ignorance in using it; secondly, whether the false direction which I might have given to the play of the right-hand finger was the cause of it, or whether, by pressing that string with the left-hand, the force of the arm might not have added to that produced by the pressure of the fingers against the thumb, and, in consequence, the finger-board or neck having yielded backward, brought the string too near the frets. Very frequently I have found it proceed from one of these two causes, and I have endeavoured to correct myself of what I considered a fault.

POSITION OF THE INSTRUMENT.

Having had no master, I have been obliged to reason before raising any maxim into a fixed principle. I observed that all masters on the pianoforte agree in sitting opposite the middle of the key-board, namely the middle of the horizontal line passed over by both hands. I considered this precept very just, because, leaving both arms equally separated from the body, no motion would be confined. Hence I concluded that the middle part of the string (the 12th fret) should be found opposite my body. This opinion I found supported by the form of the guitar, which, describing the curve B C D A F, fig. 6, indicates the point A as that which should be placed on the right knee; but as in this case the instrument is too low for the left hand to be placed in the way which I find necessary, instead of requiring the guitar-makers to make any innovation in the instrument, I saught a support for my right foot which, by keeping my knee higher, raised the guitar to a proper height for the left hand. Yet, in proportion as I have required more and more of the instrument, I have found it necessary to have it better fixed in its position, from which it should not deviate but when I wished. To effect this, I have found nothing better than to have before me a table, presenting one of its corners opposite the 12th fret, allowing me to rest the point

Fig. 6.

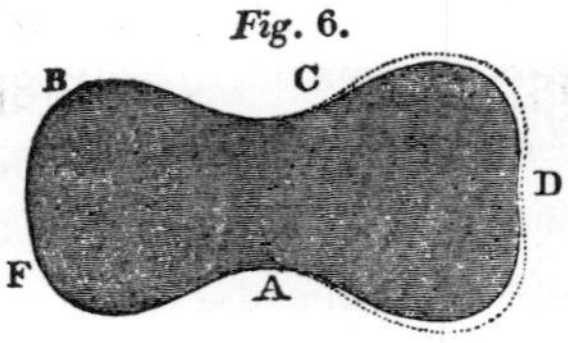

Fig. 7.

Fig. 8.

B of the instrument on the right knee a little turned out, and the point C on the corner D. By these means, finding myself placed in the position represented in figure 7. I am enabled to pass the left hand readily over the finger-board, it not being obliged to support the neck of the instrument, because the guitar is not only supported by the knee and the table, but is fixed by the weight of the right hand, which I cause to rest entirely on the point E.

I made yet another reflection on the position of the guitar. I remarked that the French and Italians generally held it in the way represented in fig. 8; and that the line A F was always parallel to the plane on which the man appears to the eye. That position (if I endeavoured to take it) would oblige me to advance the right shoulder in a constrained manner. My arm, having no support, could not determine a fixed position for the hand. The tendons acting continually to keep the arm in an unnatural position, such as the angle B C D, would make me feel difficulty in moving the joints of the fingers, and indeed often pain. At first I said to myself that this position could only be compared to that of a pianist sitting at one end of the key-board; that the left arm being raised for a long time, the circulation of the blood must be affected in the parts most distant from the body; that the line C D, formed by the fore-arm indicates its continuation D E as the natural direction of the right hand, and that the latter being obliged to rise to encounter the strings, the wrist must be in a continual state of contraction in

Fig. 9.

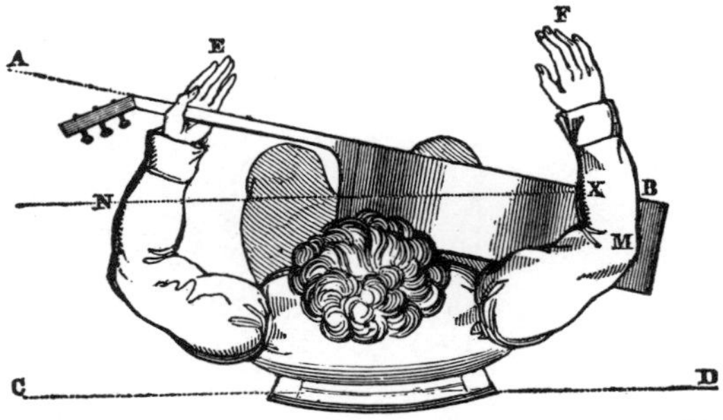

order to keep it curved. I establish as a principle that since on my left I should have only the hand beyond the line A B, fig. 9, whilst on my right, half the fore arm should be advanced, the line A B could not by any means be parallel to the line C D, if I wished to prevent displacing my right shoulder, and the parallel could only be N B. Thus placed, I found that by letting my right hand F incline naturally, it came exactly in front of the strings; that, from its form and the different lengths of the fingers, I could use to advantage the dimensions given it by nature, instead of modifying them in order to accommodate them to the proper distances; and that the point X, at the middle of the fore arm, serving me as a support, I had only to make a motion with the elbow to cause the arm of the lever X M to act in the opposite direction to that which I desired to communicate to the other arm of the lever X F.

RIGHT HAND.

The line on which the strings bear at the edge of the bridge, is a straight line, as well as that of the nut, consequently all the strings are in the same plane. If these strings were to be touched by keys or moved by quills, like the old harpsichords and spinets, all the hammers or jacks (when not set in motion) would be seen to form a straight line parallel to the strings which they were to set in vibration; and when several were made to act at once, they would always preserve a straight line parallel to the plane of the strings, and this would be one cause of uniformity in the quantity and quality of the sound. From this truth I deduced that it is necessary for the ends of the fingers of this hand to be placed in a straight line in front of the strings and parallel to the plane which they form, and I examined whether my fingers were found in that situation naturally. I saw that my fingers did not allow me to apply a straight line to touch the extremties of more than three of them, fig. 10, A B, and that if I wished to bring in the fourth, it would always be at the expense of the two which, being obliged to be bent not to over-pass the line E A (the others continuing extended), would place my hand in a constrained position, on account of the difficulty which I have always experienced in bending one single finger (excepting the thumb), if the others have not a point of support, as happens to the left hand. The joint of the thumb as well as its position cause its action to be in another direction different from that of the fingers, and, besides the possibility of pushing the string, it can approach them or recede without deranging the hand. It can slide on two succeeding strings with such a velocity as to make them both be heard together. I therefore establish as a rule of my fingering, for the right hand, to employ commonly only the three fingers touched by the line A B, and to use the fourth only for playing a chord in four parts of which the part nearest to the base leaves an intermediate string, as in example 1, Plate I.

Fig. 10. *Right hand.*

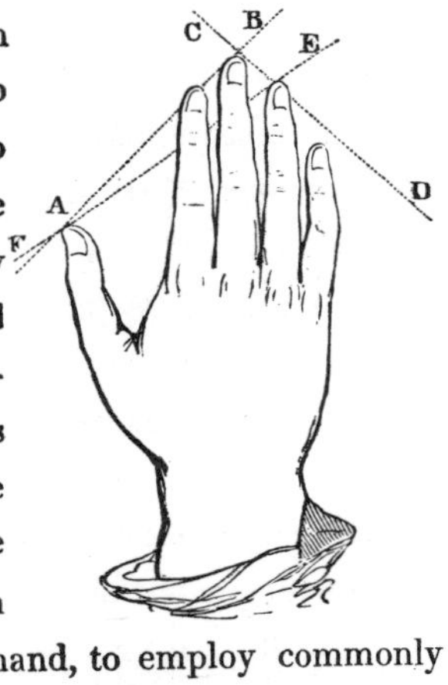

The fingers in front of the strings should not be more curved than those represented in fig. 11. The act

Fig. 11. *Right hand.*

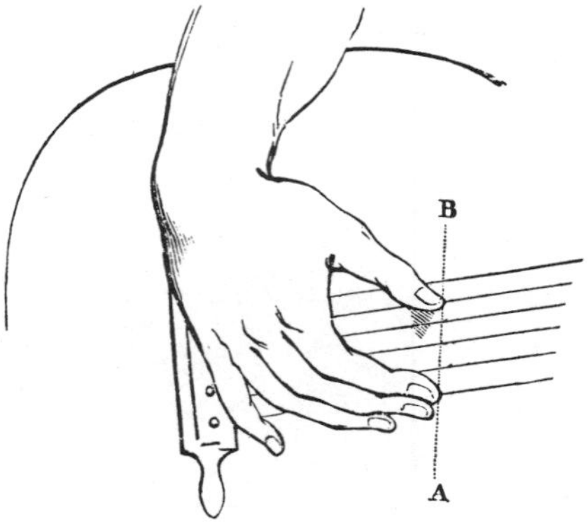

of setting the string in vibration ought to be only the act of shutting the hand, without however shutting it entirely. The thumb should never be directed towards the hollow of the hand, but act with the next finger as if going to make a cross with it, going itself above the finger. To keep the line A B parallel to the plane of the strings, I found it necessary to raise the hand a little on the side of the little finger. Many other precepts I imposed on myself with regard to the right hand; but as its position alone is the matter in question here, I shall speak of them when treating on the quality of tone and the manner of setting the strings in vibration.

LEFT HAND.

This hand has occasioned me to make many more reflections than the right. I observed that most guitarists had only half the hand before the finger-board, because it sustained the neck, with the summit of the angle formed

Fig. 12. *Left hand.*

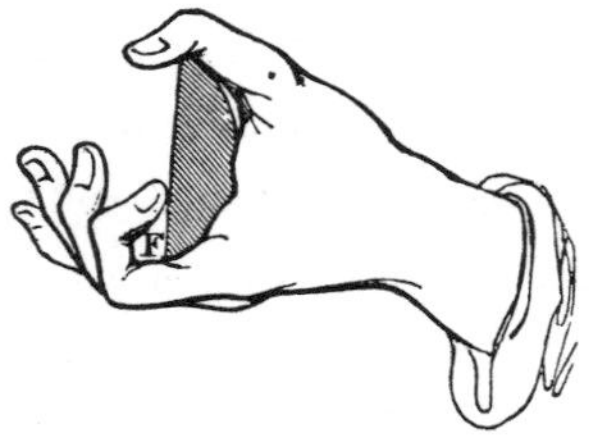

Fig. 13

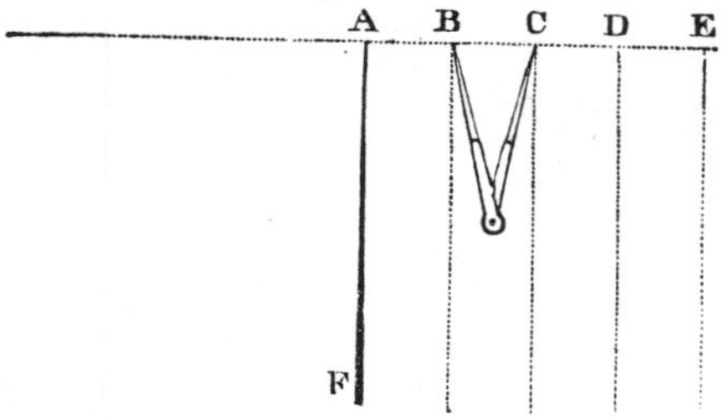

by the thumb and forefinger, fig. 12; that in this position I was obliged to contract the forefinger excessively to press F at the first fret of the smallest string; that the ends of my fingers not falling perpendicularly on the strings, I must make greater efforts to press them, and consequently it was almost unavoidable to touch the neighbouring string and to damp a sound which I might want; and when I had to perform a note a semitone higher than that which was within reach of my finger, it was necessary to displace my whole hand, which I could not do without displacing likewise the fore arm; and I could not acquire a perfect assurance of finding again the point desired, when removed from it, if my whole arm was to concur in the action, because if I ought to be sure of taking the distances A B, B C, &c. (fig. 13). exactly, I could never be so certain by using a stick E A, as by employing the small pair of compasses B: the length of the former and the want of a point of support occasion the end of it to be more liable to variation than the points of the compasses.

All these inconveniences were motives sufficiently powerful with me not to place my hand in that manner. I saw no reason why the thumb, which plays such an important part in the right hand, should do nothing in the left hand, except on occasions wherein nature having given it neither the suitable form nor dimensions for that employment, it was to play a very different part from that which was intended for it. I therefore began by supposing, as an established principle, that being shorter than the fingers, and having the power of acting easily in the opposite direction, it might be brought to meet them, and offer a point of support for the neck, the profile of which in section

Fig. 14.

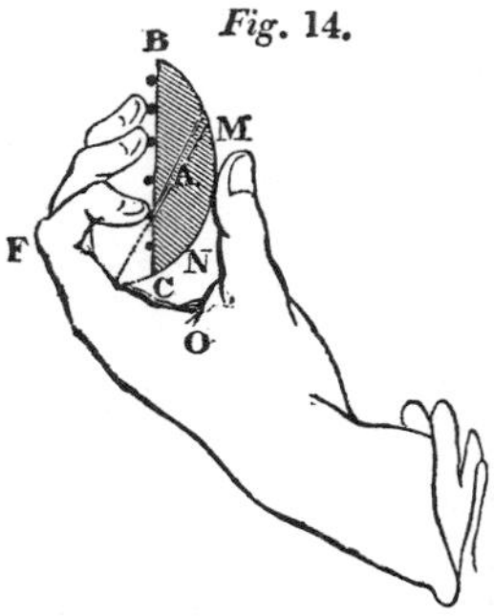

is represented by the segment A, fig. 14, so that the neck might not yield to the pressure of the fingers. These fingers being to fall perpendicularly on the strings, the position of the forefinger F gave that direction to the extreme joints. By unbending the finger indicated, I could, without the least difficulty, reach the point B. By placing the extremity of the thumb M on the point N, I could place that of the forefinger on C, without being obliged to contract the joints in so violent a manner as if the neck were supported at the point O; and, finally, I employed the thumb as it is used on the pianoforte, namely, as a pivot on which the whole hand changes its position, and which serves as a guide in returing to the position quitted. Then it was that, astonished that performers had not availed themselves of all these advantages, I inquired the reason of a guitarist of some celebrity, who replied, that the hand placed in the way that I indicated, was deprived of the use of the thumb for the sixth string, and, taking up the guitar, he played the phrase shewn in the second example, plate 1, saying: "how would you do this, without using the thumb for the first two notes of the base?" "I would not play it in any way," I replied; "first, because I would never make the base and the upper part proceed by direct octaves; secondly, because I should never terminate a perfect cadence by an inversion, instead of the direct chord," as he had done; "and thirdly, because I could not press a string with the thumb without contracting my shoulder, without bringing my hand behind the neck (and consequently annulling in a great measure the play of the fingers shortened by one half), and putting the wrist into a position far from easy, in order that the tendons which should actuate the joints may have the room and direction suited to the liberty of their action."

He answered my fourth reason only, and still in a manner which could by no means rectify my ideas, if wrong. "This is quite indifferent to me," said he; "every one has his own way, and provided he plays well, it is no matter how he may set about it." "It appears to me, however," I replied, "that if my setting about it in the best manner should influence the facility of my play, that would be worth the trouble of finding out. I am almost persuaded that I have found it; but not presuming to be infallible, I earnestly seek for well-founded objections."—"Sir," added he, "I give lessons only to my scholars. Your knowledge of the scientific part of music, leads you to disdain submitting to the precepts of a guitar-master. Besides, you are but an amateur, and whatever you may do will be thought charming in society, and genteel among artists; but if you had in view to become a professor, you should take a master; and, if I had the honour of being selected, I should set you to practise the scale, requesting you to make no remarks to me on the rules established by men whose knowledge of the subject far exceeded yours, as well on account of their long study, as of their *experience;*" and he laid great stress on the last word. I perceived, with regret, that my first two reasons had excited his displeasure, much more than if he had comprehended them, and that he could not forgive my sixteen years, for having allowed me time to occupy myself with a thing to which he was a stranger at forty. I added, again, that, persuaded the gentlemen of whom he had spoken had not established their rules blindly, the best way of paying respect to their merit would be to prove its superiority. Containing himself no longer, he said, "It is not at my age that one can be examined by a boy." The persons present blamed his precipitancy. He felt the reflections made to him in support of what I had said. He was convinced that he had been in the wrong, and he held out his hand to me. My tears flowed for joy. Returned home, I endeavoured to correct the phrase which he had played to me, and I discovered the method of doing so without the assistance of the thumb, in the manner exhibited in the third example. I contrived other deviations, and found that there are some which cannot be performed at all with the thumb, such as those of the fourth and fifth examples, and which I played readily enough with the hand placed as in fig. 14. This experiment induced me to establish it as a principle to place the thumb always at half the width of the neck, facing the finger which answers to the second fret; never to displace it but for the purpose of barring, which I effected easily, if, instead of making great efforts that all parts of the finger, fig. 15, should touch all the points in the line A B (the width of the finger-board) with a force capable of pressing them

Fig. 15.

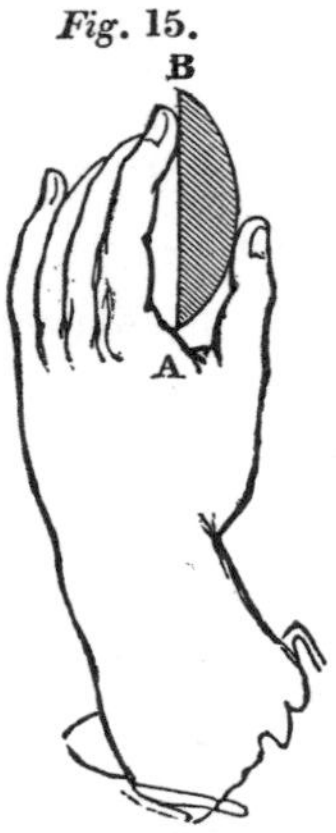

Fig. 16.

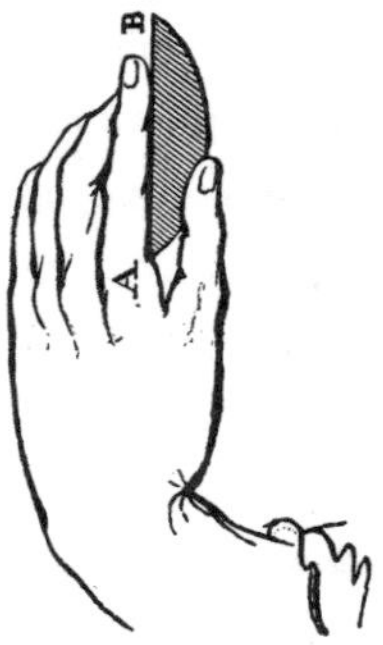

against the fret, I withdrew the thumb towards the edge A, fig. 16, and giving the fore finger the direction of the straight line A B (a line which, by its construction, cannot be bent in the contrary direction), I regarded only the support of its extremity, B, and that of the thumb; and not to press, in any other case, the thumb against the neck, but that it might be the approach of the arm, which, conducting the hand beyond, might experience a check to advancing farther than necessary, by the obstacle which the thumb would offer in opening as far as possible. In few words, let the thumb not seek for the neck, but let the neck meet the thumb.

THE MANNER OF SETTING THE STRINGS IN VIBRATION.

In speaking of the left hand, I have said, that when a string jarred, before attributing the cause to a fault in the instrument, I examined whether or not the fault was in myself. I began by establishing a principle which nobody can dispute, namely, that a stretched string, as soon as any agent whatever causes it to quit the strait line, towards which it is strongly impelled by its tension, if that agent ceases to prevent it, will fly towards it with an impetuosity which will carry it beyond the line on the opposite side; and this deviation will in its turn produce a similar effect, this alternation continuing in proportion to the difference between the force of impulsion received and its tendency to repose. I should, therefore, consider my finger as an agent which moves it from its natural position, and that the direction in which my finger moves it will determine that of its reaction. By giving to my finger the form of a hook, fig. 17, the act of touching the string would be that of directing it towards the point B. Reaction carrying it necessarily towards the point C, it would strike against the finger-board, and jar against the frets. This friction, besides being disagreeable, being an obstacle to the freedom of vibration, must diminish the number of vibrations, or the duration

Fig. 17.

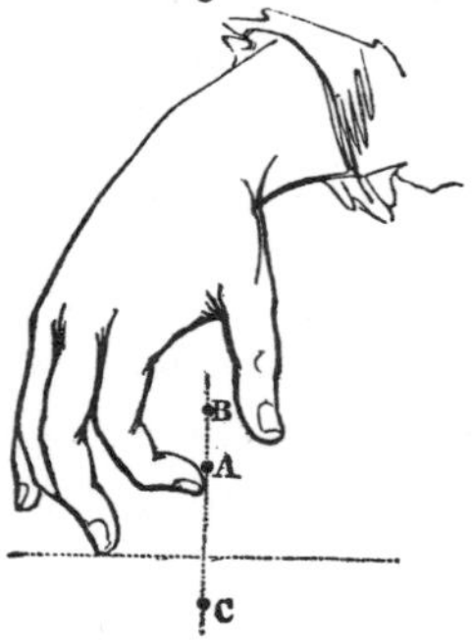

Fig. 18.

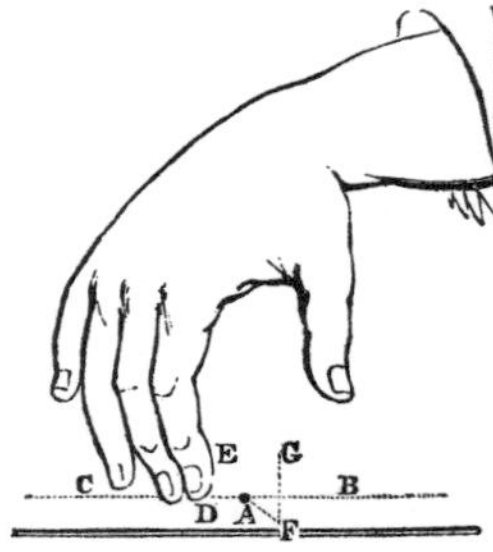

of the sound. This induced me to establish as a principle from which I should never depart, to keep my fingers as little curved as possible, for the following reason:—by supposing A the size of the string (fig. 18), the fore finger, in moving it, communicates the impulse towards the point B. The reaction must take place towards the point C, and the alternate motion having been once established, the vibrations would take place in a direction parallel to the plane of the sounding-board, as well as to that of the finger-board, and the equidistance would be always preserved, It is true, that the roundness of the tip of the finger, which tends to make itself a passage, causing the string which presents itself as an obstacle to yield to its impulse, will compel it, through the curve D E, to take, at the same time, the direction towards F, which will produce the reaction F G; but the space in which these vibrations will take place is much smaller, and the first vibration meeting with no obstacle, the sound will be pure, and will continue as long as the goodness of the string and the instrument will permit.

QUALITY OF TONE.

It is not sufficient that an instrument be well constructed; the strings must be of a suitable size for it, and must be tuned to the pitch answering to its dimensions, in order to judge of the quality of its tone.* The guitar-maker, Manuel Martinez, of Malaga, on receiving an order for a guitar, after having made a note of the dimensions desired, always asked: " Do you string it with large or small strings? Do you like a silvery or soft tone?" And he regulated his proceedings according to the answer. Thus I have seen guitars which did not give satisfaction, but which, as soon as I had furnished them with proper strings, excited surprise by the favourable change. But I speak, in this place, only of the manner of producing the tone. The stretched string offering more or less resistance, in proportion as the finger applied to it is nearer or farther from the bridge, the vibrations must be made with a different velocity (not different frequency) in every point of the half of its length, and the resulting tone should be likewise different. I thought that, in order that the instrument might yield me all the gradations of piano and forte, I might not make those gradations depend on the hand alone, and so avoid such inconveniences as touching one string instead of another, or playing two strings instead of one, or missing those which I intended touching. I wished to take advantage of that difference offered by the string on touching it in different places, and I established the common place of the hand at one-tenth of the whole length of the string from the bridge. At that point, its resistance being nearly as powerful as the impulse given to it by my finger, without a great effort, I obtained a clear and lengthened tone without its being violent. When I desire to have a more mellow and sustained sound, I touch the string at one-eighth part of its length from the bridge, profiting by the curve A B, forming the inside of the extreme joint (fig. 19) to make the sound result from a kind of friction, and not from a pull. If, on the contrary, I desire a louder sound, I touch it nearer the bridge than usual, and, in this case, I must exert a little more force in touching it.† Sometimes, indeed,

Fig. 19.

Fig. 20.

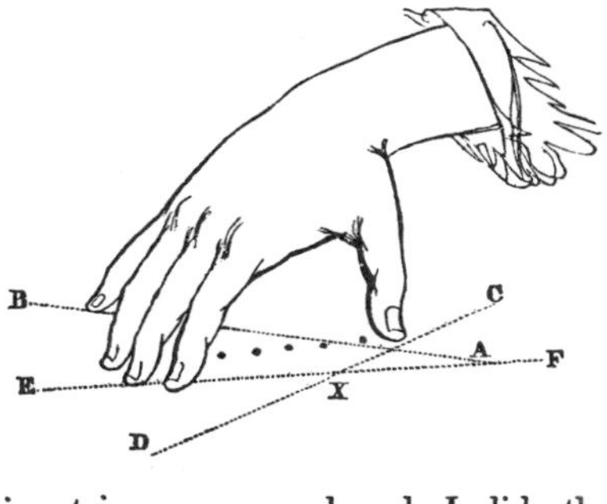

when I would play with force a chord in which all the six strings are employed, I slide the thumb across them all with rapidity, taking care that its direction be parallel to the sounding board, without which I should run the risk of

* If you tune a little guitar up to concert pitch only, you will have a real kettle.

† See M. Young's Enquiry into the Sounds of Strings.—Tr.

missing the latter strings, if I took the direction of A B, fig. 20, or of forcing them too near the point X of the sound-board E F, which would make them jar against the frets. I never make the quantity of tone, in this case, depend on the pressure of the thumb against the strings. I know that the blow received by a plane from a solid body falling upon it, is more or less, according to the height from which it falls. This force is called, in statics (dynamics?), the quantity of motion; and this quantity of motion is the product of the weight of the body, multiplied by the velocity (or the straight line passed over in its direction) in every point wherein the body is found. This multiplication has a much greater product than if I took the gravity of the weight, and multiplied it by the total height, because the augmentation is more than in arithmetical progression. Hence it follows, that in this process, if I increase only one of the two factors, the quantity of motion will be always augmented. Considering my hand as the heavy body, and the line passed over by the thumb as the velocity, the quantity of motion (or momentum) will be the product of the one by the other. Instead of increasing the weight of the hand, by adding the impulse of the arm, I so manage as to prevent that from taking place: I leave the wrist at liberty, and increase the velocity in passing over the line of motion, which I begin at a much greater distance from the sixth string than that where I generally hold the thumb.

The imitation of some other instruments is never the exclusive effect of the quality of the sound. It is necessary that the passage should be arranged as it would be in a score for the instruments I would imitate. For instance, the horns might very well perform the sixth example, plate 1; but that melody not being natural for the second horn-player, who would be obliged to employ his right hand to produce B, it is written as in example the seventh. This phrase being already in the style, and, as it were, in the dialect of the instruments that I would imitate, I have already given a direction to the illusion of my auditors; and the quality of the tone resembling that of the horn as much as possible, I increase that illusion to such a degree, that it adds whatever is wanting to the reality. I should avoid producing a silvery and tinkling sound, and, in order to succeed, I take no note with the left hand on the string to which it first belongs, but on the following string contiguous to it, so that I do not play any open string. In the passage, example 8, I should never employ the first string: I should play E with the second, C with the third, &c.; and I should touch them a little farther from the bridge than the sixth part of the whole length of the string.

The trumpet has passages which are seldom given to any other instrument. These passages are commonly all in the intonations, shewn in example 9; so that, in playing little phrases in the style of example 10, by touching the first string with force, near the bridge, to produce a tone rather nasal, and by placing the finger of the left hand, which is to stop the note on the middle of the distance, between the fret of that note and the one preceding, I should obtain a jarring noise, of very short duration, sufficiently imitating the rough sound of that instrument. To obtain it, I must take great care to press the string well against the finger-board, for every note that I play; but, as soon as I have done so, I should diminish that pressure a little, that the fret B, fig. 21, near which my finger should be found in every other case, may allow a greater length of string to enter into vibration: then the string, M C, jarring against the fret B, which first made it produce the note, will yield a harsh sound at the commencement; but that harshness will immediately cease as soon as the intonation or pitch is fixed (as happens with the trumpet), because the distance of the fret O B from the bridge, being considerably longer than B C, the latter cannot entirely prevent the vibrations of the string, which would continue from the point B.

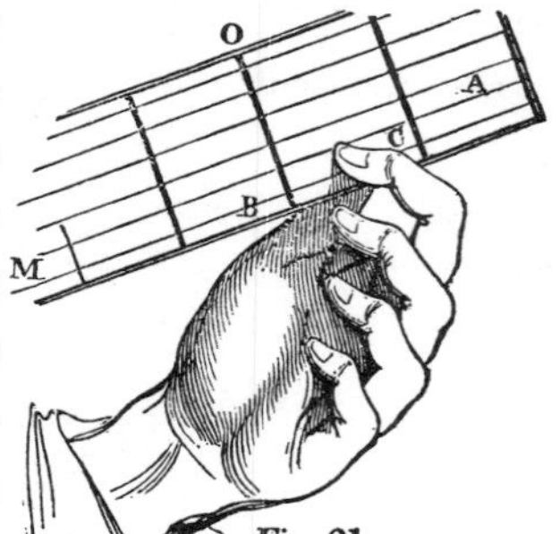

Fig. 21.

It would be impossible to imitate a singing passage for the hautbois, and I have never thought of venturing on any others than short passages in thirds, intermixing slurred and staccato notes.

As the hautboy has quite a nasal sound, I not only touch the strings as near as possible to the bridge, but I curve my fingers, and use the little nail I possess, to set them in vibration; and this is the only case in which I have thought myself able to employ the nail without inconvenience. Never in my life have I heard a guitarist whose playing was supportable, if he played with the nails. The nails can produce but very few gradations in the quality of the sound: the piano passages can never be singing, nor the fortes sufficiently full. Their performance is, to mine, what the harpsichord was in comparison to the pianoforte—the piano passages were always jingling, and, in the fortes, the noise of the keys predominated over the sound of the wires. It is necessary that the performance of Mr. Aguado should have so many excellent qualities as it possesses, to excuse his employment of the nails; and he himself would have condemned the use of them if he had not attained such a degree of agility, nor found himself beyond the time of life in which we are able to contend against the bend of the fingers acquired by a long habitude. His master played with the nails, and shone at a period when rapid passages alone were required of the guitar, when the only object in view was to dazzle and astonish. A guitarist was then a stranger to all other music besides that for the guitar. He would not, indeed, hear any other. He called the *quatuor* (quartett) church-music; and it was from such a master that Mr. Aguado received all the principles which have directed the mechanism of his play. But he felt good music himself, and, from the time when he began to act without any other guide than his own exquisite taste and his own understanding, he inclined, as much as he could, towards a more musical style than that of other guitarists. Mr. Aguado had justice done him: he acquired a certain celebrity, which his excessive modesty induced him to think of very little importance. It was at that time that I became acquainted with him. He no sooner heard some of my pieces than he studied them, and even asked my opinon of his playing; but too young myself, to think of openly blaming the way of teaching of a master of his reputation, I but slightly pointed out the inconvenience of the nails, especially as my music was then far less removed from the fingering of guitarists in general than it is at present, and, by taking a little more pains, he succeeded in playing all the notes very distinctly; and if the nails did not allow him to give the same expression as I did, he gave one peculiar to himself, which injured nothing. It was only after many years that we met again, and he then confessed to me that, if he were to begin again, he would play without using the nails.

As to harmonic sounds, I do not think that they can always imitate the flute, because the flute cannot produce sounds so low in pitch as the guitar; and, to imitate an instrument, it is requisite for the imitating instrument to be at the same pitch. No man can well imitate a woman's voice, if he does not sing with a falsetto, because the two natural voices are at the distance of an octave apart.

Music for the guitar is written in the G clef; but, unless devoid of every degree of reasoning or accuracy of ear, nobody will dispute that a string of the same size, equally stretched, and half the length of another, will sound an octave higher; and every person admits that E of the open first string of the violin is not that of the first string of the guitar, which has the same size and tension, and double the length. The real E of the guitar is that of the first line of the staff in the G clef. But, once admitted that it plays an octave lower than the notes, that makes no difference in regard to performance. It is necessary to pay attention to the notes to which the harmonics correspond; for if I would imitate a flute, I should never succeed by producing the passage as it appears in example the eleventh, but by producing it at the height of example the twelfth—not such as the guitar commonly yields the notes, but such as they are in the general scale or clavier.

Buffed sounds, or sons étouffés, I rarely employ. I have always too much regretted that there was no method of giving more sound to the instrument, in order that I might occupy myself with the methods of diminishing it; yet, as these sounds, properly employed, may produce a good effect, I have endeavoured to distinguish them from the full sounds: the latter have only the resonance damped, while the former are damped in the very act of moving the string. To damp or check the sounds, I have never employed the right hand; but I have placed the fingers of the left hand so as to take the string on the fret which determines the note, pressing it with less force than usual, but not so lightly as to make it yield an harmonic sound. This manner of damping, or buffing, requires great accuracy in the distances, but produces true suppressed sounds.

For staccato sounds, also, I do not more employ the right hand, but I merely cease pressing the finger-board with the left hand, without quitting the string as soon as it has been played: I do not impose even this task on the whole hand, the thumb alone answering the purpose, by a slight effort, almost imperceptible.

Lastly, to imitate the harp (an instrument of similar tone), I construct the chord so as to comprise a great distance, or interval, as in example the thirteenth, plate I., and I touch the strings at one-half the distance from the twelfth fret to the bridge, taking great care to have the fingers which play them depressed a little between the strings, in order that the friction of the curve D E, fig 18, may be more rapid, and produce more sound; it being understood that the passage is in the style of harp-music, such as that of example the fourteenth.

All these differences in the quality of the sounds produce a good effect, if not employed too profusely; and, with respect to learners, I would advise them not to practise them at all, until they have acquired great certainty with the common quality, as well because those varieties have always been for me exceptions to the fundamental rules which I have established for my right hand (and it is only the stabiliment of the rules that can prevent my being misled in the exceptions) as because these exceptions themselves would not produce the desired effect, without the assistance of the rules.

I should not, perhaps, have spoken of the imitation of instruments till the end of this work; but it appears to me that I ought to insert in this article every thing relating to the quality of tone. If I have not spoken of harmonic sounds, it is because I considered that I ought to treat of them in a separate article, having much more to say respecting these sounds than the others. Besides, the fingering of the left hand, and the order in which the intonations are produced, being entirely different, I did not practise them till after having acquired the principal habitude; and I again repeat that I by no means say what must be done, but only what I have done, and for what reasons.

KNOWLEDGE OF THE FINGER-BOARD.

I suppose the reader to be a musician, otherwise he will find many things unintelligible in the following explanation. I make a great distinction between a musician and a note-player. The former is he who, considering music as the science of sounds, regards the notes only as conventional signs representing them, and which by the sight convey the result to the mind, as letters communicate words, and words ideas. The latter is he who considers it the science of notes, who attaches great importance to their names, the real acceptation of which is unknown to him, and who waits to be able to understand them for the period when he shall study harmony; meanwhile seeing them only as so many orders to play such or such a key of the pianoforte; to press such a string with such a finger, in such a place, on the violin, violoncello, guitar, &c.; or to open or shut such a key, or so many holes, of the clarinet, flute, &c.; and it is the instrument which first conveys to his head, through the ear, the result of all the combinations of notes. The note-player succeeds, by dint of practice, in making an acquisition, which is to music what the motions of a rope-dancer are to dancing: he considers an isolated sound, how it is named, and to what key of the pianoforte it corresponds; but, while guessing at it, frequently it happens that he sings out of tune, as it might happen to a rope-dancer that, with all his equilibrium, he might not be able to make a regular pirouette on the floor. I shall, by no means, undertake to give a treatise on music: what I might say respecting it, in a work wherein I should principally keep in view a different object, would be insufficient to form a musician. Besides, explaining merely the reflections which I have made for my own guidance, as I was a musician before making those reflections, and as it was music that served me as a basis for all those I am about to publish, I ought to suppose the reader in the same situation as I was myself.

The frets are wires crossing the finger-board at regular intervals, which, by shortening the string one-seventeenth ot its length, raises the pitch of the sound a semitone higher. Now, by knowing how the guitar is tuned, the knowledge of the intervals of the diatonic scale should indicate to me the place where I should press the string to find the intermediate sounds between the two open strings. Example the fifteenth, plate II.

The clef not being accompanied by any sign that takes away the character of the fifth * from the note to which it gives this name, I consider it under this relation, and I perceive that the sixth string E *(mi)* is the third note of the scale of the key in which I am. From this note to the fourth (F) is a semitone, then by pressing the string at the first fret, it will produce the F (or *fa)*. From the fourth to the fifth is a whole tone: every fret being only a semitone, I must shorten the string two frets for a whole tone; I must, therefore, press the string at the third fret to produce it, and the diatonic intervals between E and A being filled up, I shall follow the same reasoning, having for basis the arrangement of the diatonic scale, which will enable me to find the frets in all the keys, without being obliged to load my memory with all the flats and sharps at the clef. See the application of it in the sixteenth example, plate II.

By the preceding example, it is obvious that, the first note once determined, I have only to observe the proportions of the intervals, and as the flats and sharps with which the clef is accompanied have no other object than to preserve the same proportion in every key, it is found that, by a single operation, I obtain a result for which I should have required twelve different ones, if, instead of thinking about what I was doing, namely, playing the scale, I thought about the names and the modifications of the notes composing it.

The true knowledge of the scale is the key to all musical knowledge; but it must be observed that to understand it thoroughly, and merely to be acquainted with it, are two different things. That knowledge is indispensible in regard to harmony; but, although this science furnishes me with great resources for the formation of rules, I wish to avoid everything that could be comprehended by harmonists only; and I shall confine myself to writing what will not require greater knowledge, in regard to the scale, than that of the proportion of the intervals. See the arrangement of them in the seventeenth example, plate III.

This arrangement exhibits the scale divided into two halves, of four notes each, wherein the order of the intervals is the same in both. These two parts are separated by the interval of a tone, and their last intervals are a semitone. The eighth note serves me as first in ascending, as the first serves me as eighth in descending; and I find everywhere the same proportions. From these circumstances, I infer where I am to find my notes, and the rules for fingering them. For example, I would run over the whole extent of the instrument: having four fingers in front of the finger-board, and my little finger being shorter in regard to its neighbour than any other finger, I cannot employ it for continuing the line A B, fig. 22, not being parallel to the strings; but, being able to use it in the continuation of the lines C D, E F, I consider it as a very useful means of keeping in position, since it can, without displacing the hand, stop all the notes that the third would have to stop by shifting. I therefore reckon but on three fingers to proceed over a straight line, without shifting the position of the hand: 1st, 2nd, and 3rd, or 1st, 2nd, and 4th. These fingers include but two intervals of a semitone; and by adding that of the open string to the first fret, I have three intervals of a semitone. Hence I establish the general rule always to use the immediate finger for a semitone, and never for a tone, and to make the fingers follow the order indicated by the frets. Example the nineteenth, plate III.

Fig. 22.

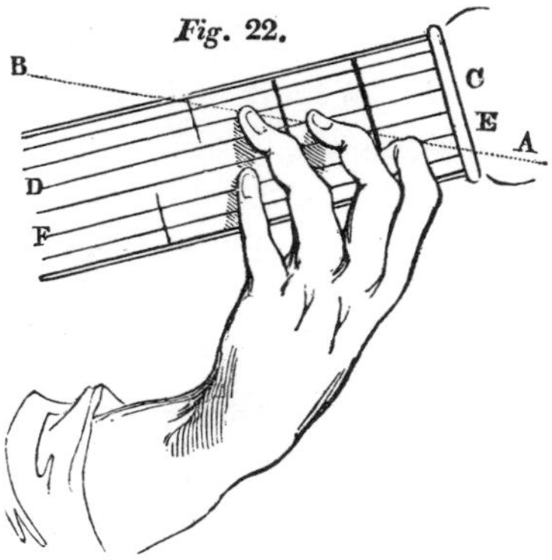

By this example it is evident that I advance but one finger when the string ascends a semitone, and two fingers when it ascends a whole tone. It is likewise obvious that when the string is to yield more than three notes, my hand changes position, and, at every change, it is found that, my fingers embracing three intervals of a semitone, I employ them according as the arrangement of the scale requires.

FINGERING ON THE LENGTH OF THE STRING.

As a sound of the same pitch may be produced by a lower string than that which I have indicated in the preceding example, I think it useful, in order to become perfect in the knowledge of the finger-board, to acquire the

* The signification of the word *sol* (or G), in the real language of music.

habit of passing over every string for the whole length, considering the open string under different relations—namely, as tonic, or first note of the key, as second, third, &c. by practising the following exercises: example the nineteenth, plate III. The fingering marked in these exercises is not the only kind I make use of; but, no matter in what other manner I finger, the hand being once in position, the order of the fingers always follows that of the frets, unless there be a necessity for making three notes, including two intervals of a tone, upon the same string. In this case, I finger them 1, 2, 4, to make the extension from 1 to 2, rather than from 3 to 4.

By playing these exercises with facility, but without rapidity, not only is a knowledge of the finger-board acquired, but also another great advantage quite disregarded in the modern way of sol-fa-ing, which leaves the care of it to the harmony, the only master, as it would appear to me, in solmisation at present existing, as I understand solmisation: this advantage arises from considering every note with respect to its place in the key, and not as an isolated sound, of which I have no idea indicating any musical relation otherwise than by ear.

USE OF THE FINGERS OF THE RIGHT HAND.

I have already explained, in the first part, the reasons which induced me to lay down, as a general rule, to employ commonly but three fingers. In consequence, I always hold my hand elevated, so as to enable the thumb to pass over four strings, and the other two fingers in front of the other two strings, so that, without shifting the hand, I may find the strings which are to produce the notes of the twentieth example, plate V., which is only the detailed expression of a chord.

This fingering has for its object, not only to economise as much as possible the number of fingers, but to make my operation conduce to the expression of the musical accent, which is nothing else than the commencement of each of the aliquot parts of the measure. The exercise, example the twenty-first, as music, differs in nothing from the preceding; but, if my opinion were referred to, I should very particularly recommend the learner not to practise it till after having acquired great certainty in the other, because the two fingers having already acquired the habit of always answering in a uniform manner to the motions of the thumb, would experience greater difficulty in choosing the moment wherein each should answer to it. But that habit once acquired, the other exercises will no longer appear difficult.

I shall speak of the use of the fourth finger when I shall have developed all the resources that I have discovered with the three.

FINGERING WITH BOTH HANDS.

Having in view, in the fingering for the left hand, not only the distribution of the fingers, but to hold the hand in a position to facilitate the performance of chords with it, I have made the latter my principal object.

I propose to myself the progression of harmony in the twenty-second example, and by disposing the hand in consequence, I find myself prepared to play the six exercises of that example.

With respect to the right hand, there would be a great number of different combinations to be made, but I have purposely suppressed them, first, because I here present only the methods which lead others to play as I do, and because combinations, like those of the twenty-third example, lead from, instead of towards, the desired object, and for this reason—I must not only have employed the fourth finger, but very frequently, although the weakest, it would have been obliged to play the accented notes; in the second place, because I consider the multiplicity of notes in the continuation of a chord only as a method of supplying the want of duration in the sounds of the notes composing it, or of imitating an orchestral passage, every part of which might have its intonations divided into small fractions, as in example the twenty-fourth, plate VI.

I employ this method, also, for imitating passages wherein the air or principal melody proceeds in notes, each of which constitutes, at most, a time of the measure; the base accompanying it with notes of the same or less value, while the intermeditate part marks the fractions of every time of the measure by notes completing the harmony. In example the twenty-fifth, there is no essential note that is not rendered by the guitar.

In general, all those variations of chords called Alberti bases, or *batteries,* if they represent nothing but themselves, have always appeared to me to produce the effect of a continued rolling, insupportably monotonous. Even when performed with true musical expression, so as to imitate the twenty-sixth example, they would only offer me something that has no expression by itself—an accompaniment; and it is only by adding the air, written above the first violin part, that these arpeggio passages can produce a good effect. But still it is necessary that he who plays it should himself forget, as it were, that he is playing an air, and should bear in mind only the object whose portrait he would present to me, namely, the score, otherwise the resemblance cannot possibly be found in it, all his attention having been engaged on the position of his hand, and the number of the strokes of his pencil. I mean that he must think of the score as a painter thinks of the object that he would represent, supposing him to know how the painter ought to consider the subject; otherwise he might paint a very correct figure, and make, at the same time, a very bad portrait.

"You wish, then," some one will say to me, "that, in order to learn to play on the guitar, I should previously learn to compose for an orchestra?" I wish nothing whatever. I state how I have reasoned in order to guide myself alone, and my playing is the result of my reasoning. At the age when I made all these reflections, I had not written any work for the orchestra, but I remarked that the movements which the guitar could render, by the arpeggio passages before mentioned, were never those of the first violin, but almost always of the second; that the celebrated Düssek had the texture of the orchestra in view when he wrote for the pianoforte the passage in example the twenty-seventh, plate VII.; and, finally, that very frequently the orchestra itself did not, in the movements of the second violin, produce so many notes as I heard in the arpeggios of guitarists. These passages, to a certain point, I forbid. Am I wrong or right in doing so? I know not, but I have done so; and the reader may judge better than I can, by my last compositions, whether that prohibition has been favourable to me or injurious. If what he may find in them is not equivalent to what may yet be wanting, certainly I have been in the wrong. Yet, as this work bears the title of a Method, a title which engages the author to give his opinion on whatever the instrument can produce, even though he might not execute it himself, I promise the reader to give him advice on the subject, which will direct him towards the end he may wish to attain.

It is by being familiarized with the preceding exercises that I think it proper to commence practising the diatonic scale to the extent of one position. For instance, in the scale of C, example the twenty-eighth, by fixing the third finger on the base, the first, second, and fourth will be very naturally in the scale up to G, without deranging the hand.

As to the right hand, I have never aimed to play scales staccato, or detached, nor with great rapidity, because I have been of opinion that I could never make the guitar perform violin passages satisfactorily, while, by taking advantage of the facility which it offers for connecting or slurring the sounds, I could imitate somewhat better the passages of an air or melody. For this reason, I play only the note which commences every group composing the passage. In the passage, example the twenty-ninth, I play the first of the slurred notes, and as I hold the fingers of the left hand in such a position that the extreme joints may fall perpendicularly, their sudden pressure occasions, (besides the state of vibration in which the string is found,) that the stroke against the fret made with force, in consequence of that sudden pressure of the finger, still encreases the vibration, which continues after the new length of string has been so determined, producing the note which I required. I confess that I should not have been sorry to practise the fingering which produces the detached notes, at the time when I was forming my principles: the motive preventing my doing so was, that, being obliged to move my whole hand over the width of the finger-board, I should have established a system of shifting entirely in contradiction to principles of which the results gave me no cause for dissatisfaction. To play three scales detached, example the thirtieth, using the fingering of guitarists, I must have the first and second finger on the first string, afterward on the second, third, and so on successively to the sixth string, so that my hand would be found quite out of reach of the strings, as represented in figure 23. I could not take this position without displacing the arm, (and by so doing increasing the difficulty of returning again with certainty to the

Fig. 23.

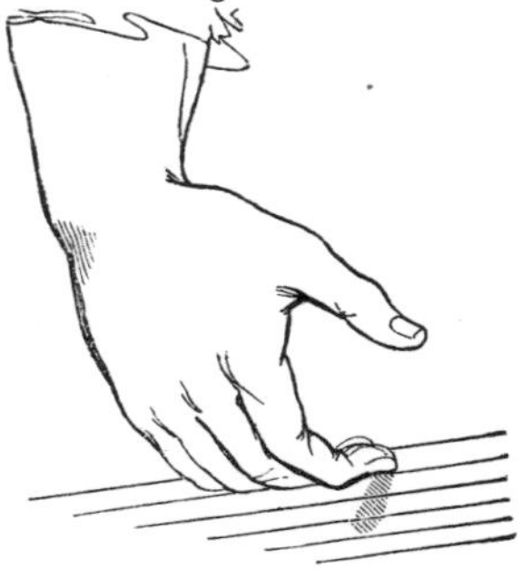

Fig. 24.

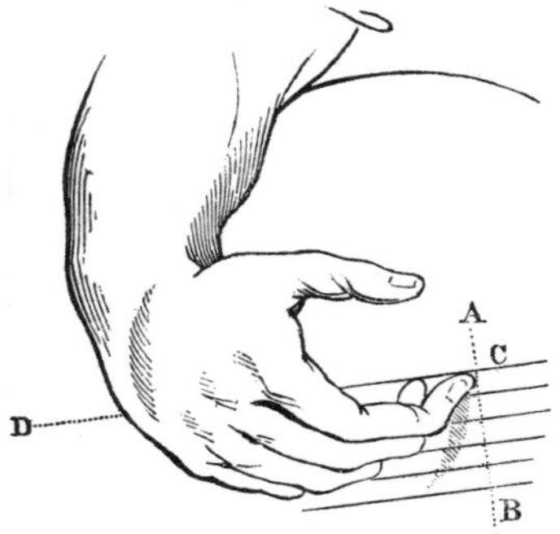

position wanted,) or by bending the wrist, in the manner represented in fig 24, which would render it impossible to play the string without the action of pulling it up, because the direction of the fingers in their natural play is not indicated by the line B A, but by the line C D, and before making the finger act in a direction lateral to that which is allowed by the joints, I must make the whole hand act, in order to give it the necessary direction for setting the string in vibration. Nevertheless, as it would be possible, by dint of labour, to succeed in acquiring facility in recovering that of the two positions which I had quitted, I forbid the latter only (either according to figure 23 or fig. 24), because I derive incomparably greater advantages from that exclusion than from the exclusion of that which I have adopted. I know that the fingering for detaching notes is reduced, to employ two fingers alternately on the same string. Sometimes I thus employ them, but never on other strings than the first, and, very rarely, the second; and never but for a single repetition, and on unaccented times of the measure, reserving the thumb for the accented notes. See example the thirty-first.

Should the reader wish to learn to detach notes with rapidity in a difficult passage, I cannot do better than refer him to the Method of Mr. Aguado, who, excelling in this kind of execution, is prepared to establish the best rules respecting it.

OF THE ELBOW.

The left elbow has, likewise, been the object of my reflections, because its position having a great influence on, or rather being the cause of, the direction in which the fingers press the strings, I have judged it proper to guide it by methodical and well-founded rules.

The position which I commonly give to it is such that the fore arm lies in a direction which, from the point whence I observe it, appears perpendicular to the neck. It requires no more than to be initiated in the elements of geometry to comprehend that, if one straight line cuts another, the alternate angles are equal, the internal equal to its opposite external, and the two angles of the same side equal to the sum of two right angles. *

The joints occasion the fingers to shut in the same direction as they open, and this direction being the continuation of the fore arm, can only be perpendicular, as well as the extreme joints of the fingers in bending towards the

---

* The establishment of this principle should be allowed me, as well as whatever proves other kinds of knowledge than those composing the education of a musician: these have enabled me to reason, and I communicate my reasonings to the reader. It has never been considered ridiculous in the authors of various musical dictionaries to fill their explanations with radical signs, $\sqrt[3]{ab+cf}$, $\sqrt[3]{\frac{ac}{b}\times x}$, &c. they might, perhaps, employ another method of explanation; as for my own part, I have no other method.

strings, This, again, was a reason for my forbidding the position of figure 8, page 10. In order that the extreme joints of the fingers might fall perpendicularly, it was necessary for me to raise the elbow to a height at which it was impossible for me to support it more than two minutes. If I depressed it, the fore arm making an acute angle with the neck, the direction of the fingers (the complement to two right angles) formed an obtuse angle. The joints causing the fingers to bend in the line of their direction, they fell on the strings in an oblique direction, forming, with the upper part of the finger-board, an acute angle, equal to its alternate angle, made by the fore arm and the finger-board. That inclination deprived my fingers of their power, because the articulations exerted their resistance in a lateral direction; and if I wished to increase the pressure, I was obliged to bring the elbow close to my body (which I could never do without contracting the shoulder), and the greater were my efforts, the less power I possessed in my fingers; for the alternate angle becoming more acute, by the approximation of the elbow, and the line of the fingers deviating more from the perpendicular, the pressure was weaker. The elbow, as I commonly place it, allows of being moved from or towards the body, according as the chord may require. In the second half of the sixth measure, plate XXXI, I am obliged to bring it near the body, that the little finger may be found naturally near to the sixth string, to press it at the fourth fret. In this case, the second finger is the pivot on which the hand turns. For the commencement of the following measure, I not only direct the elbow towards its usual position, but raise it higher, that the tips of my second, third, and fourth fingers, may be found naturally in a line parallel to the frets. Most passages that appear difficult, cease to have that appearance as soon as the elbow takes the proper position. To bar, for example, I must vary according to the position in which I bar; for the object being to give the first finger a direction parallel to the frets, and the action of its joints not allowing it any other motion than towards the thumb, which I hold facing the second finger, I must necessarily close the angle formed by the fore arm and the neck, and, consequently raise the thumb towards the first finger, in order that the latter may form a line parallel to the fret. This line is so much the more nearly parallel, in all its points, as the finger presses the strings a little more laterally. Some person will say, "It is not worth while to tell me what I do already without thinking about it, nor to use for explaining it all this train of mathematical expressions." A language is often spoken, and spoken sufficiently well, without the speaker's being a grammarian; but as soon as it becomes a question to examine its principles, it is necessary to have recourse to grammar, and especially to logic, if the object is to teach it; for without a good classification of ideas, there can be no perspicuity, nor precision, in the explanation. The citizen gentleman had made prose during forty years, without being aware of it. This idea, which Molière employed very appropriately, is, unfortunately, too often interpreted in a way to encourage and perpetuate ignorance. It was not science that Molière designed to turn into ridicule, but pedantry, or rather those who, confined and isolated as to mechanism, and entirely strangers to the purpose, attach a great importance to their minute knowledge. The other interpretation is in fashion, because it is the only arm that ignorance employs against reasoning.

I have detailed, in this second part, all the reflections that I made, and the reasons which led me to establish the principles which have always served me as a ground-work; but I have not yet said anything relative to music. I have observed that most methods begin where I begin the third part, without treating at all on the two articles which form my first two parts, excepting the table which exhibits the sounds of the open strings, and the frets where the others are found. I can attribute this omission only to a desire to reserve explanations, which I think indispensible, in order to give them to learners only orally. For my part, seeing differently, I think a pupil would be less discouraged by reading what he should do, and, in the absence of the master, to become his own guide, than to be interrupted every moment during the lesson by such observations as, "Bend the left arm. Do not contract the shoulder. Your left hand fingers do not fall sufficiently perpendicular: those of the right hand are too much bent. Your guitar is turned too much: you do not touch the string at the proper point, &c." The instruction would be somewhat slower at the commencement; but, after a very little while, it would proceed with rapidity. It is true that there are scholars who consider him the best master who has to make observations most constantly: "He takes so much trouble!" say they; but I do not in the least doubt that even they would be much better pleased to have it in their power to say—"He has nothing to correct but mistakes in fingering, or in the manner of considering this or that phrase." The master, on his part, besides having much less need to put his patience in requisition, would derive greater credit from his labour, and, I believe, even more profit; for if a scholar attained, in less time, sufficient skill to do without taking his lessons, the example would encourage those who hesitate to begin, through fear of being fatigued, for a long period, by arid principles and exercises, the real object of which they cannot perceive. Rules, not given from authority merely, but with the reasons for which they were established, make a better impression received by persuasion than by memory; for, certainly, to say, "I do such a thing, because I have been told to do so," has not the same force as to say, "I do such a thing, because in being advised to do so, I have been shewn the reasons for it, and I perceive its intention and utility." I have always said to my pupils, whether in singing or on the guitar, "When I direct you to observe this or that precept, never rely on my authority merely, but inquire the reason; and if I have none sufficiently convincing to satisfy you, it should greatly diminish the confidence with which you honour me in regard to the science.

OF THIRDS, THEIR NATURE AND FINGERING.

Beginning with the deep strings, the diatonic intervals between the sounds of the six open strings are three fourths, a major third, and another fourth; and, as by pressing two or several strings at the same fret, they should include the same intervals as the strings do when not stopped, I conclude that, since by pressing two strings at the same fret they produce a fourth (excepting the third and the second, which produce a major third), if I raised the lower of these two strings a semitone, by pressing it at the next fret, I should produce a major third; and, by pressing it again at the following fret, I should produce a minor third. I therefore tried to play over the scale in thirds, by establishing one mode of fingering for the major and another for the minor thirds, and I considered that of example the thirty-third, plate VIII. the best. Besides the advantage of keeping the hand always well placed, I also found that of playing the scale in thirds in every key, without thinking about the notes which I was playing, or of the flats and sharps by which some of them were affected. For example, the scale in D flat, major key:—this note, once determined, I knew that its third (F) could only be major; the second note should be a tone from the key-note, and its third should be minor; the third note should be again a tone from the second note, and its third be minor also; the fourth note should be a semitone from the third note, and its third be major, and so on. Now, when the key-note is on the second string, the third above it being on the first string, I fix in my mind the formula which follows the example referred to.

This formula is invariable, as long as the tonic, or key-note, is found on the second string: by placing my second finger on it, and my first finger on the first string, I have only to follow the order of the diatonic intervals for the distances from the first finger (which ought to slide along the string), and to press the second string with the second finger, if the third is major, or with the third finger if it is minor; for the sharps or flats at the clef having no other object than to enable me to find the diatonic scale everywhere, in all its proportions, as soon as I considered the notes under their musical relation, I should find my thirds more promptly than by considering them under a mechanical relation. To know the nature of them, it is unnecessary to learn that the major third consists of two tones, the minor third of a tone and a half; that the diatonic scale, in the major mode, has three major thirds and four minor thirds; that the major thirds are produced by the tonic, dominant, and subdominant, and the minor thirds by the submediant, mediant superdominant, and leading note. It is necessary merely to know the proportion of the scale, and, by examining the thirty-sixth example, it will be seen that the third, which includes one of the small intervals, must be minor relatively to the third, which contains whole tones. All the learned catechism just mentioned will be for the reader but a natural consequence of what the example offers to his view; and, as he will himself discover it, his memory will receive a more lasting impression, for conviction has a very powerful influence in making it. Let a long speech, in Latin, be given me to learn by heart, I should be much longer before being able to recite it, than if it were in French, English, Spanish, or Italian, because it is a language with which I am less acquainted. Not being sure of comprehending the meaning of every phrase, I should learn most of the words like a parrot, and my memory receiving no aid from the understanding, might very readily be found at fault; but let a good latinist explain to me the construction and the meaning, and I should experience the same facility as in the other languages.

For the thirds produced by the third and second strings, the relation of the fingering should be different, because these two strings are tuned a major third to each other: all the major thirds will be produced by pressing them at the same fret with two fingers, or with one finger only; and the fingering employed in producing the major third on the other strings, will produce the minor third on the strings in question.

By example the thirty-fourth, it is seen that it is only requisite to direct the attention to the distances to be passed over with the second finger, which never quits the third string, and to give every note its corresponding third. If the same notes were found in the key of E flat, I should not at all embarras myself with the notes which must be played a semitone lower, and those which must be natural: I should perceive that G is the third of the transposed key, by considering it under this relation I should say that its third, being required to be minor, cannot be played on the second string, and I should play my first two notes after each other (supposing, in this case, that only the two strings in question are under consideration), the following note is then the fourth, and its third is major. The fourth note being only a semitone from the third, I should find it at the first fret, as well as its third, &c. Thus, by following the order of the intervals, and the nature of their thirds, my fingering will enable me to produce the notes properly modified, without my being obliged to stop to consider the minutiæ of their modification, and I should play in the manner indicated in the thirty-fifth example, plate VIII.

For the thirds which occur in the compass of the fourth and third strings, or of the fifth and fourth, or of the sixth and fifth, their nature and the disposition of the hand have always shewn me the right fingering, by observing the principle of employing, only in very rare cases, two following fingers for a minor third. But, before exhibiting the general table of thirds in all the keys, I ought to communicate to the reader an exercise which I prescribed for myself, as soon as I was fully convinced of the necessity of acquiring the fingering of thirds. This exercise, as soon as learnt on two strings—the second and first—is learnt on all those which are tuned to the interval of a fourth. It is reduced to considering the sound of the lowest in every relation to the scale or key, and, consequently, to continue along the whole length of the finger-board. See the thirty-seventh example.

Having once accounted to myself for this fingering, I experienced not the smallest difficulty in establishing that of the scales in thirds, in all keys, and throughout the whole compass of the instrument, as will appear in the table, example the thirty-eighth, plate IX.

After perfectly comprehending the preceding table, a few exceptions, in regard to the fingering of thirds, remain to be explained, and I shall, in this article alone, have already explained half the theories constituting my system of fingering, as far as concerns chords.

Minor thirds, the fingering of which is denoted $\frac{1}{3}$, should sometimes be fingered $\frac{1}{4}$, if they are accompanied by a base which requires the second finger, and $\frac{2}{4}$, if the base requires the first. A trial of the thirty-ninth and fortieth examples, plate X, will shew by the natural position of the hand, that I have always consulted the length, the form, and the articulations of the fingers.

When the thirds are among the deep sounds, it is sometimes necessary to use the fingering $\frac{1}{2}$ for a minor third, if the little finger is employed at a considerable distance from the first; for the third being shorter and weaker than the second, it is more natural for the second to extend from the first, than the third from the fourth. In the second strain of the religious march in Mozart's Magic Flute, (Zauberflötte), a passage occurs, example the forty-first, in which the thirds should be fingered according to example the forty-second; but, as the little finger is obliged to support A, I have been obliged to finger according to example the forty-third.

There are still other exceptions, but I have promised a faithful explanation of the progressive steps by which I have obtained from this instrument results which have deserved the approbation of connoisseurs; and I have never ventured on too bold exceptions, till after having contracted a habit of the general rules, and, as it were, having identified myself with them.

OF SIXTHS.

I knew that all plain chords contain a third at least, (either between the base and one of the upper parts, or between two upper parts), or a sixth, excepting the discord of the fourth and fifth, which I consider as a retardation of the third.

Having established my system for thirds, no more was necessary for me to do than to establish one for sixths, in order to have a positive rule for the fingering of all chords imaginable. I shall not relate all the reflections that I made on the subject, because I should not be understood but by harmonists, and because, as long as I can avoid a language not comprehensible by every body, I shall not employ it.

I saw that two following strings gave me a fourth, or a major third; and that each of those which gave me a major third, formed a fourth with the string next to it: see example the forty-fourth. Now, by leaving an intermediate string, these four strings form, in consequence of the way in which they are tuned, two major sixths: example the forty-fifth. Consequently, if I play together the fourth and the second, the third and the first strings, open, or stopping them at the same fret, no matter which, they will produce major sixths; and by raising the lower note a semitone, namely, by stopping a fret in advance of the highest, they will produce a minor sixth. I observed that the conformation of my fingers saved me the trouble of seeking for the fingering; because they were found naturally arranged, and all that was to be considered was to pay attention to the kind of sixth belonging to every note of the key.

This knowledge gives the greatest facility to him who would in some degree know music, as music, namely, as the science of sounds. He knows that the octave includes two intervals, one smaller by half than the other; and that these small intervals are between the third and fourth and between the seventh and eighth notes. The sixth, because including six notes, must sometimes comprise one, sometimes both, of the smallest intervals, according to the notes of the scale forming the sixth; wherefore, having the construction of the scale as a point of comparison, we can never be deceived as to the nature of the sixths. The sixth which includes one of the smaller intervals, will be major, * and that which includes two will be minor. See example the forty-sixth.

My fingers, placed naturally, offer me the fingering of a minor sixth and of a major sixth.

If the phrase, example the forty-seventh, contains four of them, it is because I profit by those which are produced by the open strings. Now, by employing this fingering, I am enabled to play over the scale through the whole extent of the finger-board, and I shall do so as it is fingered in the forty-eighth example.

If my attention be directed towards the lower part, I have only to consider what note of the key it is, and what kind of sixth belongs to it; and, if carried towards the upper part, what it is, and above what note is it a sixth: I then pass over the scale musically in sixths, in every key, with the same facility as in thirds.

On the practice of thirds and sixths the whole of my fingering depends; and I cannot too strongly recommend the study of it to those who would execute my music without the appearance of difficulty, a display of which is forbidden by good taste, For the rest, to move the fingers too much, by separating them farther from the frets than is necessary to leave the string at liberty, is to augment the difficulty; and I have always preferred hearing it said of a performance, " He appears to be doing nothing, that appears so easy;" than to hear it said, " Oh! how difficult that must be! for he appears to have given proofs of it." This is one of the reasons why the greatest pianists will never forget Cramer, Field, Kalkbrenner, and Bertini.

---

* As the minor third will be that containing one of the minor intervals, and the major third that which does not contain one.

Plates XI and the following contain exercises which, well studied, include my whole method in regard to harmony.

APPLICATION OF THE THEORY OF THIRDS AND SIXTHS.

The reader will have remarked that the fingering for thirds and sixths differs sometimes from that which I have indicated in the general table. On playing those passages he will find the reason which determined me to make that difference. He will perceive that I have endeavoured to avoid, as much as possible, the transition from one string to another with the same finger, and, in particular, that I have been sparing in the shiftings of the hand.

He who shall have adopted my method, and, having approved my reasons, learnt to play the preceding exercises, may be certain of possessing every thing that serves as a foundation for the performance of my music. It might be considered that I advance too much, if I did not prove my assertion by the analysis of some musical piece, and that task I shall undertake. In these exercises, although he should have already perceived how many useful results proceed from this mode of fingering, he will perceive still more on studying the exercise, plate XVI, containing both methods of fingering. *

I cannot in the least doubt but that this exercise will fully convince the reader that, with the knowledge of thirds and sixths, it would be possible to finger all the most difficult guitar music, and, consequently, perform it in such a way as to indicate that the base and other parts of the harmony proceed in a regular manner. I return, therefore, to speak of myself. As soon as I found myself in a state to play thirds and sixths through the whole extent of the finger-board, I endeavoured to apply them, by proposing to myself a succession of chords. See example the forty-ninth, plate XVII.

I perceived that for the first two chords I had only to make the base and its octave for the first, and the upper part for the second, because the other notes belong to the open strings. In the third chord I observed a major sixth, B flat, I fingered it $^{4}_{3}$, and the second finger fell naturally on E. In the fourth chord I fingered $^{1}_{2}$ the sixth, A F, and the third finger with the second made me the third, F A. In the fifth chord, I observed a major sixth, C A, which I fingured $^{4}_{3}$; and seeing E flat above C, forming a minor third, and having already the third finger on the third string for producing C, I had only to let the second finger fall to make this third, and the first finger was prepared to stop the F sharp, which is the base. † In the sixth chord, I observed a minor third, B D, belonging to the third and second strings, and I fingered it $^{1}_{2}$. I likewise observed a major third, G B, the upper note of which was already made on the third string; the fourth string was, therefore, to sound the under note, and I made it with the third finger, as shewn in the general table. For its octave, G, forming the fourth above D, which I stopped with the fore finger, I had only to take the first string; and as it is when an open string, the fourth above the second string, being pressed at the same fret they must preserve the same interval.

The seventh chord is like the fifth, only it is a tone higher in pitch.

The eighth chord contains the inferior third, A D, which is minor, and belonging to the third and second strings; I should, therefore, have fingered it $^{1}_{2}$, and the first string open would have given me with the second string the major third, C E; but this first string being employed in making the lower A, I must take the thirds on lower strings: I took A C on the fourth and third, fingering them $^{1}_{3}$; E being the major third above C, which I stopped with the

---

* I shall not forget the analysis which I have promised; but as in a piece of music there is melody, and as the fingering employed by me is almost always dependant on that which should serve me for harmony, I shall speak a little more at large on the latter, and after having explained the rules which I myself observe for the former, I shall keep my word.

† Having promised to employ only such expressions as are not exclusively reserved for harmonists, I shall not here mention the names of the chords; but shall speak of them when I compose a treatise on harmony applicable to the guitar.

first finger, must be found on the same fret, as well as its fourth A. Now, by taking the three strings with the first finger, I produced the chord in question.

The ninth chord contains the major third A flat C. Having to play the C an octave above that which forms a third with the lowest note, I took it first with the fourth finger, afterwards I fingered the base and its third $\frac{1}{2}$, and the third finger very readily made the note F a major sixth above the base.

The tenth chord contains the major sixth, D B, which I fingered $\frac{4}{3}$. F is the minor third from D, which I held with the third finger on the third string, I had, therefore, only to let the second fall naturally upon the second string, and I had all the parts of the harmony of G, a base which the first finger made easily on the fourth string.

The eleventh chord offered me the major sixth, F D, to which I applied the proper fingering, $\frac{4}{3}$, and the second string open gave me the note B. Not being able to give G in the same way, because the third string was employed in producing F, at the tenth fret, I produced in on the same fret with the fifth string, which, yielding its octave A at the twelfth fret, should necessarily produce me G at the same fret where I made F D.

In the twelfth chord, the minor sixth, E C, and major third, C E, indicated to me their fingering, according to the general table.

The thirteenth chord is like the seventh, and the fourteenth like the eighth.

The fifteenth chord contains the minor third, E G, which I should have fingered $\frac{1}{3}$, if I had not had any note to stop with the second finger; but being obliged to employ it for making C sharp, I fingered the third $\frac{1}{4}$, and for B flat, as the G which I held with the first finger is its major sixth, I extended this finger and made that sixth with it.

The sixteenth chord contains the major third, D F sharp, the fingering of which should be $\frac{1}{2}$; but the first finger being employed for A, I used $\frac{2}{3}$, and the fourth open string gave me the base.

The seventeenth chord is like the fifteenth, but a tone lower in pitch, and the eighteenth is like the first.

The nineteenth chord contains the major sixth, B flat G, and by fingering it with $\frac{4}{3}$, the second finger was naturally placed on C sharp, and the sixth open string gave me the base sound.

The twentieth chord contains a minor third, D F, which I fingered $\frac{1}{4}$, because my second finger was not only employed with the first in making the minor sixth, A F, but because the first finger being obliged to bar, in order to produce the F of the base, caused the hand to advance much more, and, consequently, the fourth finger was better prepared than the third to press the second string.

The twenty-first chord contains the minor third, B D, which belongs to two strings, namely, the second and third, and should be fingered $\frac{1}{2}$. The other two notes being found at the same fret, where I held the second string with the first finger, I had, therefore, only to bar all the strings, by keeping the second finger on B, and I produced the chord.

For the last chord, the minor sixth, E C, and the major third, C E, indicated to me the proper fingering.

I have entered into all these details to prove to the reader the truth of my assertion, that the entire key to the mastery of the guitar (as an instrument of harmony) consists in the knowledge of the thirds and sixths. Without this knowledge, I believe that I should have succeeded in producing only a poor imitation of the violin or rather of the mandoline. I say *poor*, because I should have been destitute of the great advantage of the former of these instruments, that of prolonging, increasing, and diminishing the sounds; and of the brilliancy of the latter, which being, as well as the former, tuned an octave above the guitar, gives passages which the latter can but very imperfectly imitate, at least in my hands.

FINGERING OF THE LEFT HAND IN REGARD TO MELODY.

As it is very rare that I can determine to leave unproved any thing that I advance, I am about to state why it is that I almost always make the fingering which I employ for melody depend on that which I use for harmony.

I consider the scale, no matter in what key, as the perfect chord or triad of that key, commenced by the base ascending, or by the upper part in descending; and sounding successively, not only the parts composing that chord, but likewise all the notes that fill up the intervals between those parts. The fiftieth example, plate XVI, will show the reader that, by having the left hand placed for making the chord, the whole scale is found under the fingers without the necessity of shifting it, excepting the scale should exceed the compass included by the chord; and that it is the open string, or the fourth finger, which produces the complement to the parts fingered for the chord.

If the scale were required a semitone higher, example the fifty-first, the act of barring being nothing else than making a fret, against which the first finger presses the strings serve as a nut, I consider that I have only three fingers remaining disposable; and the major sixth, A flat E, (which this nut enables me to produce) serving for the chord, I finger for the minor sixth, F D flat, $\frac{2}{3}$ instead of $\frac{1}{2}$; for my second finger becomes first, and my third finger second. I observe that this F is a major third above the base, and I make it with the fourth finger, which is become third. The fingering for the chord once determined, the fingering for the scale becomes perfectly natural, and will serve me from semitone to semitone throughout the whole length of the finger-board, if the tonic (or key-note) is produced by the fifth string; but, as it is desirable to take advantage of the open strings, I have established other modes of fingering with that intention.

In the scale in the major mode of D, example 52, as the fourth string sounding the base cannot, at the same time, sound the F sharp, I place the chord over the note which gives its first inversion (or chord of the sixth and third), namely, over F sharp. I finger the third, F sharp, A, in the same manner that I finger all the minor thirds, $\frac{1}{3}$; I straighten the first finger and produce with the first string the major sixth above A, which I hold with the extremity; my second finger is enabled to make D on the second string at the third fret, which is nothing more than the fingering of a major third between that string and the first string.

In the scale of E flat, I employ the fingering according to the extent which I am to pass over. If I wish to play only ten notes, I employ the fingering of No. 1, example 53; if I wish to play to twelve notes, I employ that of No. 2 (which is nothing but the chord of C in example 50), by considering that my second note F, my fifth B flat, my seventh D, and my tenth or third G, being found at the third fret, this fret becomes the nut, and the first finger being obliged to make these notes, the second, third, and fourth fingers are to take the places of the first, second, and third, in order to play all the notes of the chord at once.

In the major key of E, by establishing the third, E G sharp, according to the fingering for a major third, the second and first string open give me the complement of the chord, and I finger the scale as shewn in example 54.

In F, I observe the minor sixth, A F, which I finger according to rule $\frac{1}{2}$, and my third finger can produce, with the second finger, the major third, F A. For the note C, forming a minor third with A, I use the extremity of the first finger, which being employed on the first string at the same fret, takes the two strings very easily. My chord thus completed, the fingering of the scale becomes quite natural, as shewn in example 55.

In the key of F sharp, the chord once formed (No. 1 of example 56), I find myself obliged to depart from the general rule of fingering, to make the interval from F sharp to G sharp; but I prefer this deviation to quitting the principal position which I must take again to make the A sharp, and I finger the rest nearly as in F natural. The scale in G flat being at the same fret, requires the same fingering. See No. 2.

In G natural, the third and second string being the first two notes of the perfect chord, or triad, of G, and having no string between the second and first to produce D, I suppress it, and I make the octave G with the fourth finger. My hand thus placed, I find my fingers within the reach of the notes I require, and, without the smallest motion of the wrist, I play the scale as fingered in example 57, plate XVIII, No. 1. I can also make the fingering depend on the chord D, A, C, F sharp, by considering the notes G, B, D, as intervals to be filled up, as in the example, No. 2.

Being able to make a perfect chord under the note which I have taken for a point of departure in the two preceding numbers, I can fill up a double extent, and make what several professors of the guitar call the grand chord. See No. 3.

By fingering the base G, and its nearest third, B, with the fingering of a major third, $^{1}_{2}$, the fourth string open giving me D, I add the position No. 1; and as soon as I have used the position of the hand for the first octave, I place it for the fingering, No. 1, up to F sharp, which I make with my first finger, in order to prepare fingers for the notes up to D, applying one finger for a semitone and two for a whole tone.

In A flat, I see only the chord of G a semitone higher; I must therefore imagine that the first fret becomes the nut, and I reserve the first finger for all the notes which, in the scale of G, are found on the open strings. I use my second, third, and fourth fingers as I should my first, second, and third, and the fingering of No. 1, example 58, is the result. If the scale is to begin an octave higher (No. 2), and is not to exceed an octave in extent, I consider it as the scale of G, No. 1, example 57. A semitone higher, I take the three strings with the first finger, I likewise place the fourth finger at the fourth fret, and the chord, once formed, I employ the fingering No. 2, example 58. If the scale is to exceed the octave, I take the chord with the same fingering that I used for all those chords, the base note of which belongs to the fourth string, beginning with F, and I establish the fingering No. 3.

In the major key of A, I stop the notes as they occur under my fingers when the hand is regularly placed; but as, after G sharp of the third string, no note is found at the first fret, when I require the second fret for G sharp, I slide the whole hand a semitone, employ the first finger (example 59, No. 1), and make the following notes depend, up to A, on the fingering No. 2. (preceding example) with this difference alone, that it is placed a semitone higher; and I take advantage of the notes produced by the open strings. If I wish to lay the chord on the fourth string (No. 2.), nothing more is requisite than to do, at the pitch A, what I have done in example 58, No. 3.

In the major key of B flat, example 60, the first finger to the base and the fourth finger to its octave, with the fourth string open, give me a position which enables my hand to pass easily over all the intervals comprised in that extent. When I exceed this compass, the act of sliding the first finger from C to D makes me advance a tone higher, and finding myself in the same case as when at the tenth note of the scale, No. I, example 58, I have only to follow the same procedure.

Lastly, in the key of B natural, the major third, B D sharp, which I finger $^{1}_{2}$, gives me the proper position for passing over the diatonic intervals up to B, the second open string. As that string has only the first string before it, it cannot be the base of a chord, because a chord should be composed of at least three notes. I continue the scale, therefore, thinking of the nature of the intervals only, for a knowledge of the frets and the suitable distribution of the fingers, and hence results the fingering in example 61.*

All passages of melody have not the same compass, the same direction, nor the same series of intervals, nor have they the same point of departure; consequently, it was necessary for me to account to myself for what I was about to do, before occupying myself about the means by which I should do it more easily. But how can a passage of melody be explained, without having recourse to harmony, at a time when solfaing is no longer the science of sounds? *Mi, sol, do, si, re, fa, mi, re, do*, plate XIX, example 62, were anciently the exclusive nomenclature of this melody; but, at the present day, the same melody has only to change its place (or pitch) to change its nomenclature (making seven names for a single thing), and this nomenclature, in its turn, becoming the expression of a greater number of different things, modern solmisation wants precision in its musical ideas, and is exclusively the science of notes, so that the explanation which I might give being fettered by the deprivation of a great many means of rendering myself intelligible, I should be obliged to employ circumlocution to express ideas which, for that reason, might appear complicated.

The only method that I see is, to request the reader to pay great attention to two very essential points in regard

---

* The reader will have found me too minute, perhaps, in this article, but I request him to take into consideration that, faithful to my principle, to establish nothing by authority, I owe an explanation of whatever I propose, and I think to shew him greater respect by submitting to his judgement the reasons which I have had for establishing this or that maxim, than by telling him, " This ought to be done, because it is my advice."

to *music:* first, that melody, example 63, is the same, notwithstanding that all the notes composing it be different, (see example 64 to 65); second, that the same notes may express a great number of different things, and that the object may change place, but not form; although notists make no difference in the way of considering them, unless it be the dfficulties with which the imagination is loaded, in order to convert the mind into a machine. This may appear contradictory; but it will be found, on reflection, that the whole understanding being exclusively engaged in cutting the stones composing a building, only a machine remains for the conception of the general architectural plan. It will be objected to me, that, as the general plan belongs to the architect, and not to the stone-cutter, so the knowledge which I require belongs to the harmonist, and not to the mere reader of music; but in this case he should be called a notist, and not a musician, because music is the science of sounds, and I shall never call him a musician whose ear is his sole guide in the musical part of his solmisation, but him whose solmisation is the art of classing, and rectifying the ideas which should guide the ear.

The first thing that I examine in a passage of melody is, whether it skips through such intervals as are found between the parts of a chord, or proceeds by conjunct degrees, ascending or descending; whether it ascends by groups of two or three descending notes, or falls by ascending groups. As soon as I perceive notes forming a broken chord, I place the fingers for that chord. When the notes are otherwise disposed, I finger them agreeably to their progression, according to the examples plate XVII and XVIII, and when notes succeed in the order of the scale, I observe the fingering shewn in examples 65, 66, 67, 68, and 69, of plate XX.

Moreover, I see that my first finger placed on the second string, no matter at which fret, so disposes my hand, that the fourth finger falling naturally on the first string, produces me a minor sixth, and, by extending it a fret, it easily produces me a major sixth. I have, therefore, a positive datum for establishing this position for all passages of melody that do not exceed that compass; but the fingering of the intermediate notes being changed, according to the note of the scale made by the first finger, the employment of the other fingers depends on the way in which that note is considered. I cannot convey my reasoning as a musician, because I should not be certain of being generally comprehended by saying, I begin with *do*, *mi*, &c., when the reader would see B flat or C sharp, *

I should therefore detail the different combinations, by presenting the note made by the first finger under every relation that it can have with its tonic, and pointing out the fingering, example 72.

In the passage, example 73, I take the first two notes on the third string, to prepare myself in the position of the first finger on D (the fifth note of the key), in order that I may have all the passage as far as B under my fingers. Afterwards, I treat the F sharp according to its relation with the key note, I place my first finger on it, considering it as seventh or leading note, and finger the following notes consecutively.

In a passage which should be executed rapidly, it is very useful to take advantage of a position to produce the greatest numbers of notes included in it; but, in a singing passage, I have found it preferable to seek the notes where the vibrations will be of longer continuance. G produced by the first string, at the third fret, is much more durable than if produced by the second string, at the eighth fret, or by the third string, at the twelfth. There are two reasons why there should be that difference: first, the parts of the string set in vibration are shorter; and, second, their diameter increases in the ratio of their diminution in length.†

---

* Supposing I have to make the chord, No. 1, example 71, plate XX, and that I mistake by playing No. 2, some person, wishing to correct me, would say, "Make a sharp." If I supposed him to be a musician, I should play No. 3; but if merely a notist, I should understand him not to speak of the sound, but of the mechanism to produce it, and I should play the chord No. 1. A harmonist would say to me, "Make an augmented (or extreme sharp) fifth," and I should make no mistake, for, in the solfeggi which I have learnt, that would signify, "Make G (or *sol*) a semitone higher;" and, as for me *sol* would mean the fifth note of the major key in which I am playing, I should comprehend the harmonist, even without having learnt harmony.

† If, on making trial, the G made with the second string is heard very much prolonged, the cause must not be attributed to that string, but to the resonance of the third string, which having the same note below, is set in vibration as soon as another string yields a note which is found in its resonance, especially the octave and the fifth.

I therefore prefer changing position frequently, in order to produce the melody with the second and first strings, rather than to produce notes on the third and fourth strings at the lower part of the finger-board, where the vibrations would only be prolonged in case they were repeated by the resonance of the deep strings, which could not occur for all notes; and the notes, so prolonged, would render the dullness of the others more remarkable. The fingering of my Fantasia for two guitars, called *L' Encouragement* (published by Pacini), shews, in the scholar's part, how I put in practice what has been just mentioned. It will be seen how far I take advantage of the open strings in the *cantabile*, that the sounds may be lasting, and, in quick passages, to avoid shifting.

I have found it of great consequence to accustom myself to take a position embracing at need the distance of a major third on the same string with the first and fourth fingers, so that the intermediate note shall be made by the second finger, which, by its length and action, is more capable of separating from the first than the third is from the fourth finger.

To pretend that everything imaginable in music can be performed on an instrument, is, in my opinion, not at all to know the instrument. The Pianoforte, offering so many resources, could not render the effect of my twenty-fourth study for the guitar without changing its texture, because it is not within its system of fingering. It might indeed be exactly performed without displacing a single note; but that would belong to the category of sleights of hand. It should not therefore surprise, if I have not sought rules for things which I consider not witnin the domain of the guitar. Let another writer make them, let him astonish; so much the better, if he finds the means to avoid sacrificing to the things of this kind what the instrument posseses of a more advantageous and ageeable nature. For my own part, I have not felt the force of those things, nor wished to occupy myself with that which I could not think proper to acquire, until after being quite certain of possessing a mastery over everything in the style which I have thought peculiar to the guitar.* If I hear difficulties of certain pianists, I discover immediately that they have made an almost exclusive study of them; but when I hear them from Cramer, Kalkbrenner, Bertini, and others of their class, I at once perceive that they have not given themselves up to such difficulties till after having engaged for a great length of time in more solid studies.

FINGERING FOR THE RIGHT HAND.

The common position of my fingers places my first below the second string, the second below the first string, and the thumb within reach of all the other strings, without displacing the hand. If the melody is lower than the note of the open first string, I pass my first and second fingers to the third and second strings. I touch every base note forcibly with the thumb, which I likewise employ very frequently to play notes not belonging to the base, but which mark an accented part of the measure, or the commencement of an aliquot part. If the melody is doubled in sixths, I remove a little my second finger from the first, elevate the hand a little (not by contracting the wrist, but by slightly depressing the elbow), and my first and second fingers are found each by its respective string. If the intermediate part has more motion than the upper part, and the intermediate string is to be played, I always employ the first finger, because my fingers have less facility of action in proportion as they approach the fourth. It is for this reason, that, when I have a succession of sixths to make, without being accompanied by a string, I use the thumb for all the notes belonging to the fourth string, and even for several of those belonging to the third.

When it is question of a staccato passage without accompaniment, I have heard several guitarists (and chiefly Mr. Aguado) who make them with surprising neatness and velocity, by employing alternately the first and second

* A description of all the sleights of hand and extraordinary things performed on the violin by the celebrated Paganini was given in my presence, when some person inquired, " And how does he play on the violin simply without sleights af hand ?" " Perfectly," replied the very competent judge, to whom the question was addressed. From that time I considered the artist as a real colossal talent, worthy of his great reputation.

or third fingers. But having consulted the construction of the hand, I have found that when the second finger is in action, if the thumb is at rest, it is the lower part of the hand which acts, and when I set the thumb and forefinger alone in motion, it is the upper part that acts. I am aware of the reason; but instead of making a parade of the slender knowledge I may have in anatomy, I refer to the judgement of anatomists as to my assertion. The reader may make the experiment, by playing one string rapidly several times alternately with the first and second fingers. He will see that he cannot do so, without moving the third and fourth; but let him perform the same operation with the thumb and first finger, and he will perceive the lower part remain without any other motion than that which the thumb communicates to the whole hand. This observation determined me to execute passages of that kind with the thumb and first finger, and with that view I made my nineteenth lesson and my fifth study, to habituate the learner to this mode of playing. Besides, it is easier to me to find quickly the low string which I may want immediately after the passage with the thumb, having only to open the hand without displacing it, than to pass from the position indicated in figure 23, page 22, to the position in figure 11, page 12; for I always preserve the line A B, figure 11, parallel to the plane of the sounding-board. Sometimes my left hand comes to the assistance of the right in descending groups of three notes, and I finger the three at once. The finger which stops the highest, which I play with the right hand, instead of quitting it by rising, takes the form of a hook, and being withdrawn towards the palm of the hand (without varying the position of the whole hand) produces the next following note, which is found already fingered. I do with this finger what I did with the other, and it produces me the third note. From what have just explained, the reader may easily infer that, if I rarely use the third finger of the right hand for harmony, I forbid it entirely for melody. Such are the foundations on which I establish the play of my right hand. The exceptions to the rules which I observe do not occur but when the music requires them; but then the way of writing indicates the fingering that I use, unless it be in a phrase of harmony. Example 74, plate XXI, after what I have said, should be performed by passing the first finger, which has just played A of the third string, to the fourth string to make E. But by writing it as No. 2, it is obvious that the same E makes no part of the melody formed by the minims, but a separate one whose notes do not coincide with those of the base; I can therefore employ the thumb alternately for the base and for that part, keeping my hand well placed. When, in a passage in three parts, the middle part has more notes to be played than the chief melody or air, and these notes require two strings, I observe whether the musical accent be on the highest or lowest; if on the highest, my thumb plays the lowest, but if on the lowest, I play both with the first finger, which I pass from one to the other. See the same example, in which the numbers mark the fingers of the right hand. As the thumb is not reckoned on the left hand, seeing that I never have it on the finger-board, I use the same numbers for the fingers of the right hand, and denote the thumb by a small cross ×.

Sometimes I employ the little finger, pressing it perpendicularly on the sounding-board below the first string, but take care to raise it as soon as it ceases to be necessary. The necessity for that support arises from passages requiring great velocity of the thumb to pass from base notes to those of an intermediate part, whilst the first and second fingers are occupied in completing the fraction of the measure in triplets, or otherwise, when I could never be certain of keeping my fingers exactly opposite their respective strings: the little finger then retains my whole hand in position, and I have only to attend to the motions of the thumb; but, as soon as my hand can properly keep its position without that support, I cease to use it, in order that the elevation of the lower part of the hand may allow me to attack the strings with the fingers curved the least possible.

OF HARMONIC SOUNDS.

These sounds are so called, because they are the result of different intonations, produced by the vibration of the sonorous body. A stretched string set in vibration will give these sounds, corresponding to aliquot parts of its length, the more distinctly as its pitch is lower. On touching alone the last finger-key of a six-octave pianoforte, its acute major third almost exceeds in distinctness the generating sound; but as we pass up the key-board, the farther we advance towards the middle, it is perceived that the more the generating sound comes forth disengaged from every other sound. I have heard harmonics, which in Spain are called flute-sounds. I have also heard another quality of tone different from the fluty sounds, but these were of very short continuance, and being always accompanied by the noise produced by the violent action of the finger on the string which opposes its passage, I could not conceive what relation there could be between this noise and the sound of a flute; to me they had rather the effect of the Indian Marimbo.* I observed also that they were never produced but upon the seventh fret, on the fifth very rarely, but very frequently on the twelfth; that on the latter the tone was more pleasing, and of a little longer duration than on the two others; and that the latter sound which they produced was the clearest. By reflecting on these effects I discovered the cause of them. I know that a stretched string gives me a determined sound. If I put a moveable bridge, first at half its total length, the string will produce, by each half, the octave above the original sound; if I place it at one quarter of the length this quarter will produce the double octave above, and the three-quarters on the other side of the bridge will give me the fourth above the original sound; again, if I place it at one third, this third part will give me the double fifth, and the two thirds on the other side, the single fifth above: I deduce from this theory that the part of the string which affords me an harmonic sound, is not that which I touch with my right hand, but that which is between my left hand and the nut; that it is for this reason the sounds ascend as I shorten this distance, and, the vibrations dying away sooner on account of the diminution of the length, the more my hand approached the nut, the less pure and durable were the sounds. I perceived that the same finger of the left hand that had determined the aliquot part of the string was an obstacle to the vibration, and that the sound once determined, if the string was quitted immediately, it would not in vibrating produce the generating sound, but would prolong the sound produced by the aliquot part. Guitarists withdrawing the finger from the strings immediately after the last sound, this was the only sound, unless they made it expressly, that experienced the result of the described process; and my own observation led me to establish it as a rule, first, not to press the string too lightly at the point determined, but so that I could feel it well under my finger; secondly, to let the action of attacking the string with the right hand be followed immediately by that of raising the left, to quit the string and leave it perfectly at liberty to vibrate; thirdly, in proportion as the sounds to be produced would require a position nearer to the nut, to make the action of attacking the string more violent, and the pressure of the left-hand finger more powerful, without however compelling the string to approach the fret.

After having acquired the habit of producing the sounds in a pleasing manner, I regretted that there were not harmonics for all the notes. I heard of a process by which they might be produced, but, as soon as I became acquainted with it, I perceived that the contrivance could scarcely succeed. It consisted in determining the half of every length of string between the point which was to produce the sound and the bridge, by a finger of the same hand that attacks the string, whilst the other hand is employed in fingering the notes of which the harmonics yield the octaves above. Besides the double task which was imposed on me, in being obliged to measure very accurately the distance for both hands, I found the inconvenience of being forced to employ the whole of the right hand to play a single note, and that every harmonic I wished to produce, not only cost me a motion of the wrist, but of the whole arm too, and having no point of support, it was nearly impossible for me to direct my finger with certainty exactly to the middle point of every distance. At first I attributed this to a want of practice, but some time afterward, I requested the person who had communicated this discovery to me, and who said that he used it with advantage, to play me some passages in this way. I observed that he experienced the same difficulties that I did, that he played very slowly, and

---

* Pieces of very compact wood and progressively differing in length. A cord on each side holds the ends and keeps them parallel. It is a ladder, of which the cord attaching the top is long enough to allow the performer to pass his head within it. Thus suspended from the neck, he takes the other extremity in his left hand, advancing it so that the pieces of wood shall be suspended in the air, while a flexible rod, with a solid ball at one end, is held in the right hand to strike the pieces of wood, which yield different notes.

that the pressed string discontinuing its vibrations sooner than the open string, the harmonic sounds produced by this method must be less sonorous. This greatly thwarted my wishes, for I earnestly desired to be able to produce all the sounds. It occurred to me to employ the same method as on the violin, by determining the note with the fore-finger and doing with the little finger at four frets' distance, what I did with another finger on the fourth to produce the double octave. This method was a little more promising, but I always found the inconvenience of being obliged to contract the distance between the two fingers in proportion as my hand approached the body of the instrument; and even when I had succeeded in acquiring the habit of progressive contraction, I always found myself in a state of uncertainty, when the melody proceeded any otherwise than by successive degrees. It was at this period that I asked myself the following question: " Are not all the notes of the diatonic scale found in the vibration of the sonorous body? Why should I not endeavour to interrogate nature, by determining on a deep string the aliquot and even the aliquant parts of its length?"—I made the trial, and found that the fourth string, for example, gave me the following notes:—

At the twelft fret	the octave	D
At the ninth	the tenth, or major third	F sharp
At the seventh	the double fifth	A
At the fifth	the double octave	D
At the fourth	the double major third	F sharp
A little below the third	the triple fifth	A
A little above the same	the triple minor seventh	C
Below the second	the triple octave	D
On the second fret	the triple ninth	E

All these notes are not equally distinct on all the strings. Their clearness is in the direct ratio of their greater or less gravity. But, since every string affords me the same results relatively to its lowest sound, I can find on one string some note which may be wanting on another. I formed for myself the table represented by example 75, plate XXI, and I saw how many harmonic sounds I could arrange by the common method.* As some of them are almost inappreciable, I have avoided them as much as possible in my compositions; and, seeing that it was impossible for me to execute them with rapidity, in a passage of melody, without my performance bearing too conspicuously the seal of difficulty, I extended my views towards the combinations of harmony. When I play in a key the next to that of the sixth string, I tune it up or down to the tonic, or key-note, and then the harmonic sounds, preserving their relations with the generating sound, should yield precedence in regard to those of the other strings, and I find in D or F the sounds indicated in example 76 and 77. Having several places where I can find the same note, I take advantage of this circumstance to play in two or even three parts in harmonics. It would be useless to mark the fingering, because I never write the resulting note, but the string to be played and the number of the fret where it is to be pressed. The reader will see, in one of my twenty-four studies, that, by following the numbers, he will produce the three parts. I shall however present him with another instance in example 78, plate XXIII, in case he should not have my studies before him.

Sometimes I take advantage likewise of the violin-method, already mentioned, but very rarely, and with great caution. In one of my variations on Paesiello's theme, *Nel cor piu non mi sento* (Hope told a flattering tale), I terminate both strains by two sixths in harmonic sounds, example 79. It is seen that, for the latter, I fix the first finger on the fifth string, at the third fret, to determine C properly: this fret becomes the nut, and if, at five frets' distance I should produce the double octave above the open string A, I should produce at the octave (become fifth), the double octave of C. I produce the double octave of E with the second finger, on the fifth fret with the sixth string, and both

---

* It should not be lost sight of, that the guitar being tuned an octave below the music written in the G clef, the harmonics are exactly at the pitch where I have written them. See plate XXIII.

notes sound very distinctly: this variation, however, is slower than the others. I do not say that, with a great deal of practice, success might not attend the methods mentioned for playing harmonics, with greater rapidity than I can. In this case, I shall always rejoice at being surpassed, for it will be a proof of the utility of my researches.

ACCOMPANIMENTS.

In this article I cannot explain myself in the same manner that I have reasoned with myself, having promised to use only terms comprehended by every reader. Harmony and counterpoint have been my guides, but I ought to avoid whatever would assimilate me to those who prefer not loosing an opportunity of employing technical terms (even if there were other terms less mysterious), to making themselves intelligible.

Every accompaniment supposes, in the first place, a base and at least two harmonious parts; consequently, the different notes composing what is generally called arpeggio (or batterie), must not be considered as the expression of a single part. That I may be able to impart to the accompaniment the expression of that which it represents, I must make myself acquainted with the object that I desire to imitate. The base marks for me the commencement of the aliquot parts of the measure, the musical accent; but these accents are more or less numerous, according as the music has been composed. For instance, in an air in common time, counting four times in a measure, all marked by the base, and wherein the notes of the parts of the harmony being of the same value would all strike together, I should consider two notes accented, namely those designated by the odd numbers, one and three; so that the first and the third would be the accented, and the second and fourth the weak or unaccented. And, when I have merely two accented times in a measure, the second should be less marked than the first. In general it may be established, that a base has half the number of its notes accented, and that every note in a measure occupying the place of an even number, even when it would be accented with regard to the parts of the harmony, would not be so as base. For this reason, I took great care to accustom myself to play the base as I require it to be done in an orchestra which accompanies, and to give the other parts of the harmony the same degree of power as I should require of the violins, and not more; in other words, that the base should be more marked, and the parts succeeding it should be heard so as to be distinguished as dependant on the base, in like manner as resonance is less powerful than the sound producing it. This refers only to the manner of playing an accompaniment. I should like to explain how I reasoned with myself in order to form accompaniments; but, besides its being impossible, without using terms which I ought to avoid employing, this rather belongs to the treatise which I intend to publish, *On Harmony applied to the Guitar.* I shall, however, point out everything that the simple knowledge of thirds and sixths may render intelligible.

A pianoforte accompaniment, if well made, should be constructed like an orchestral quartett or trio. Now, by taking that accompaniment as a pattern, I can, thereby, regulate that of the guitar. Comparisons greatly assist the comprehension, and I request the reader to allow me one to prove, that if the guitar does not give the same notes as the orchestra, either in quantity or pitch, the accompaniment will not be less the same. If a portrait be made as large as life, it may exhibit all the smallest details that are observed in the original: this is the orchestra. Let a copy be made of this portrait in dimensions only one third of the former, a great part of the little details will be suppressed: other parts, which in the full size were developed, will be represented perhaps by a single point—the relative proportion of the features will always be the same, and although each will receive fewer touches of the pencil, the same object will be seen: this is the pionoforte. If of this copy another be made again reduced one-third, it will be necessary to make many more suppressions. A small circle of the original may be represented by a point, and yet produce the effect of the small circle; so that the means of seizing the resemblance being fewer in detail, the likeness will be perfect if the features preserve the same relative proportions; and this is the guitar. This truth established, I shall give the accompaniment of one of Mozart's airs, first reduced for the pianoforte, in a way to render the author's intention according to his orchestral accompaniment (example 80, plate XXV.). I observe that, as far as to the first time of the fourth measure, the left hand plays me the base as it is in the orchestral score, and the right hand strikes the unaccented times, as they are written in the score for the violins and the tenor; but, in the rest of the fourth measure, I see three descending thirds in the right hand and a holding note, whilst the left hand, besides sustaining the base which has marked the time, makes three thirds in contrary motion to those of the right hand. The whole of this passage is performed in the orchestra by win l-instruments. Afterward the same alternate play is resumed, and continued to the eighth measure, where there is again another phrase of wind instruments. My first care, in adapting it to the guitar, is to employ notes of the same value, to preserve the identity of movement; afterward to examine what thirds and sixths are found in the chords, in order to take them as a foundation for my fingering. If, for example, I find myself in the last chord of the second measure, where the minor third, F sharp A, being fingered $\overset{1}{4}$ on account of D sharp, which should be made by the second finger, cannot be accompanied by the B. which is found between this third and the base, without employing the second and fourth fingers for the third, the first for B, on the third string, and the third finger for D sharp on the fifth; this not being an easy position, I consider whether I cannot suppress one of the three notes, without destroying the effect; and I find that the voice continuing the B till it coincides with the base of the chord in question, I complete the whole by answering with two notes only. The end of the third measure is a chord having the preceding B for base: here I observe the third F sharp A, and the lower third D sharp F sharp, I finger the latter $\overset{1}{4}$, and for the other I consider A F sharp, instead of F sharp A, which is its inversion. This sixth, being minor, should be found at the same fret, and because F sharp is made at the second fret with the first finger, I have only to bar and it will produce me, not only the A, but also the B of the base, which is to be struck first. In the fourth measure, I perceive six parts, and, not being able to play all of them, I ought to ascertain which constitute the essential part of the phrase. If I play the descending thirds correctly, the guitar does not allow me to play the other three in contrary motion; and to suppress them would be to remove the expression resulting from that approximation, I therefore make the three lower thirds, fingering them $\overset{1}{3}$, $\overset{1}{2}$, $\overset{1}{3}$, and only the highest part of the three descending thirds, and not being able to sustain the acute E, I make the open first string to be heard after each of the three notes. The resonance of E, which I played at the begining of the measure, making part of the chord to which every one of the three thirds belongs, augments their vibrations and connects the sounds, I ought, consequently, to touch them gently, but with boldness, to produce the effect of the instruments which the pianoforte is to imitate.

The reader may conceive, from the manner in which I have been obliged to reason for this little piece, whether I had not cause to be astonished when some one told me " I play only to accompany myself." If accompaniments already made are played, that supposes a theoretical knowledge of the instrument considered as an instrument of harmony. If the accompaniments are made by the performer himself, in this case much more still is supposed, even were the accompaniment to contain only plain unbroken chords, with a correct base; I shall therefore carefully forbear promising that, with a few superficial notions of the harmonical catechism, I shall afford the means of *composing easily* good accompaniments to all imaginable airs: I should not be able, by any means, to keep my word. Mozart's air, *Voi che sapete che cos' e amor,* would compel me to enter into longer and deeper explanations than those which I employ for example 44; for that analysis refers to the fingering only, whilst that of the other accompaniment should have reference to its formation, its progression, to the reasons for considering this or that chord in one way rather than in another, and to the manner of substituting *adroitly* an inversion for a direct chord, or *vice versa.* The formula of chords on the notes of the scale would be insufficient for accompanying in a reasonable manner the melody of these four lines :—

Ricerco un bene
Fuori di me,
Non so chi il tiene ;
Non so dov' e.

And yet it would be absurd to say that the transitions employed by the author, to express the anxiety and agitation of the heart of Chérubino are deviations from the fundamental rules. On the contrary, they prove that nobody has observed the rules more constantly than Mozart; but he knew all their consequences, he possessed, as it were, all the resources, and all the oratorical turns of the musical language; and, to be able to translate it well, it is necessary to understand at least how to read it properly, which would already suppose more extensive knowledge than I could communicate in a score pages of text, and six, or perhaps ten, of examples. It requires an intimate acquaintance with a language to comprehend its double and triple meanings. The discord of the diminished seventh, * with its inversions, is, in music, nothing else than a source of calembourgs (or puns), for example:—

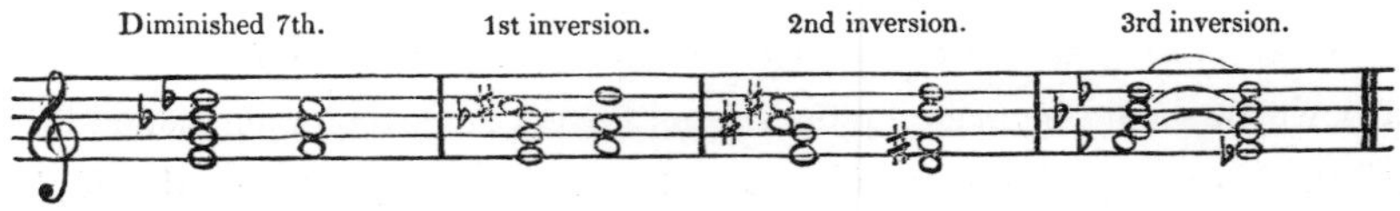

The same sounds may be considered in different relations. If I am in the key of F, and instead of giving the chord of the diminished seventh its resolution in the key, I consider it as its first inversion, I am in D minor key. If I consider it as the second inversion, I am in B minor; and if I take it as third inversion, I am in A flat major or minor key. The chord of the dominant seventh, and the chord of the augmented sixth, are likewise synonimous, and it is only their resolutions that determine their true acceptation.

I have been told that I required too much in regard to accompaniments, but it was not remarked that I did so only for airs composed to be accompanied by an orchestra or pianoforte; nor indeed that, if the accompaniments were simple, I ever thought of making them complicated by increasing the number of notes, or by harmonizing them in a more finished manner than the author had. The air of the Molinara, *Nel cor piu non mi sento*, has the greatest simplicity in the accompaniment, I would not, therefore, make any other than that of example 81, plate XXV; but how can we simplify the chords which succeed in Cherubini's beautiful romance, from the opera of the *Deux Journees*, without suppressing a great part of its merit? The voice-part is simple, touching, and perfectly suited to the situation. The orchestra has not a great complication of notes, but the texture of them is very beautiful; and considerable knowledge and tact are necessary to ascertain which notes may be omitted with least disadvantage to the effect.† I have always been of opinion, that to arrange any piece we please for an instrument which cannot render it properly, is rather to derange it; and instead of saying "arranged" for such an instrument, the expression should be "sacrificed to" such an instrument: I play the figure with a double subject in B flat in the oratorio of the Creation, by Haydn; but I should never venture to undertake Mozart's, in the overture to the Mysteries of Isis (the Zauberflötte), nor my own in that of the ballat of *Hercule et Omphale*, because the guitar being by no means suited to the nature of the subjects, nor to the treatment of them in inverted double counterpoint, I should be able to present but a skeleton.

If an air is composed to be accompanied by the guitar, I am the greatest partisan of simplicity in the accompaniment; because, in this case, all the effect should depend on the air, and the accompaniment has no other object than to mark the measure and indicate the harmony required by the base.‡ But when an air, written for an orchestra, is to be accompanied, I endeavour to arrange it as the reader will see in the portion of Haydn's Creation, (example 84, plate XXVIII. and the following) or I give it up. This is the piece of music in which I shall analyze whatever concerns the guitar, agreeably to my promise on page 27.

---

* I do not forget myself by entering into explanations relative to harmony. I use them only to prove that, if I do not give rules on the subject, it is because the knowledge of them supposes others much more profound, and because my weak abilities do not furnish me with the means of developing them properly in a few pages. By attempting it, I should incur the risk that the reader, having learnt nothing from my explanation, would conclude me to be ignorant myself of what I pretend to teach.

† See example 82, plate XXVI.

‡ See my Ariette, in example 83, plate XXVII.

ANALYSIS OF THE ACCOMPANIMENT OF PART OF HAYDN'S ORATORIO, THE CREATION.

The commencement of the symphony is a phrase without accompaniment, the first three notes of which proceed by thirds descending, the first a minor and the second a major third. I finger the second $^{1}_{2}$, and my little finger is prepared to make the upper note of the first. The E being produced by the open first string enables me readily to take C sharp with the first finger on the second string, and after having made the E following with the first string, I find myself already prepared to begin the second measure. I stretch out the little finger on the first string, which produces A, I bar all the strings with the first finger at the fret where it is found, and in that position the D sharp is found within reach of the third finger, which I slide to make E, whose major third G sharp requires the second, which I slide again to make the slurred B. I take the D with the fourth finger, and find myself already with one of the notes commencing the third measure. Among the other three notes that begin the first chord, there are two, A of the base and the B, which are produced by the fifth and second strings open; I have therefore only to make G sharp on the fourth string with the first finger, and by sliding the little finger one fret, to pass from D to C sharp, I let fall the second at the next fret, where I hold the first, in order to produce the A on the same string. For the last three notes of this measure, and the first of the following measure, although they have no accompaniment, it is still the harmony which directs my fingering. I place my hand for the minor third G sharp E sharp, which I should finger $^{1}_{3}$. The notes preceding each of these, at the distance of a semi-tone only, become very easy to me with the second and fourth fingers. In the three following chords, and in the two beginning the other measure, I observe a major sixth in each, and these sixths are alternately a semitone from each other. If there were no base to be played, or if the base were found on the open strings, I should finger the sixths $^{4}_{3}$ $^{2}_{1}$ $^{4}_{3}$ $^{2}_{1}$ $^{4}_{3}$; but the notes of the base being to be made on stopped strings, and the sixths belonging to the third and first strings, which form a major sixth as open strings, the first finger, by barring them, will always produce sixths of the same kind; I therefore make the sixth A F sharp with the first finger, and the base, to which A is a minor third, must necessarily be made with the third finger. The first finger, which by taking three strings always keeps the third and first strings in a major sixth, has only to slide a semitone to make G sharp and E sharp, which form the sixth in the following chord, and the fourth finger can make the base C sharp. I bar all the strings for the last chord, although I require but three at the second fret, not only because my first finger is already found in the proper place for the other half of the measure, but also because it has already taken the form necessary for pressing the fifth and third strings at the same fret, to produce B and A: my third finger then makes D sharp, and the second and fourth remain disposable for the motion of the intermediate part. The notes composing three-fourths of the following measure are those which form the major chord of E. The highest is an open string; G sharp is the major third of E, which I should finger $^{1}_{2}$; but as it is likewise the minor sixth of B, I finger that sixth $^{1}_{2}$, and make E with the third finger, which falls on it naturally. The chords thus arranged, I stretch out the little finger when I require G sharp on the sixth string, and and raise it for E. The two notes constituting the last quarter of the measure, and the two commencing the following, are all at the distance of a third apart. The last of these four notes being an open string, I examine what are the two intervals of a third comprised by the first three notes, and I perceive that they are minor thirds. My four fingers contain one; now I have only to take D with the fourth finger, and the first finger would naturally be found on B, I have therefore only to complete the fingering of the minor third, namely, to place the third finger on the second string, two frets more advanced than that where I keep my first finger, and I should produce G sharp. As I should be prepared to take D again at the end of the measure, to re-commence the phrase, instead of making D, B, G sharp at the high part of the finger board, I take D at the seventh fret on the third string, with the second finger; I find B on the second open string, and G at the the sixth fret on the fourth string. During E, which I make with the first string open, my hand has time to shift from the sixth to the tenth fret, to take with the little finger the note D, which begins the phrase again twice following. The G sharp commencing the second half of the tenth measure to which it is equal in duration, I make with the first finger: I turn my hand upon it and curve a little more than usual the second finger, which makes F sharp on the first string, waiting in position till sounded by the finger which has made the apogiatura G sharp. For the beginning of the eleventh measure, observing a minor sixth C sharp A, I apply its fingering $^{1}_{2}$, by sliding previously the first finger one fret, because it was found on G sharp and is to make A. The open first string and afterwards its note A produced with the fourth finger will enable me to finger the second half, by merely following the order of the intervals of the diatonic major scale. In the twelfth measure I observe four notes in succession, the first three of which belong to three successive strings pressed at the second fret. I press them with the second, third, and fourth fingers respectively, in order to reserve the first finger for G sharp, which I require after the rest, commencing the second half of this measure. The following measure begins with two notes that I could make by barring, which would prepare me for the following chord; but as I endeavour to save exertion as much as possible, I extend the first finger to F sharp, curving the second to make A at the same fret, and afterwards I finger the minor third F sharp A $^{1}_{3}$, which prepares my second finger to make D. Instead of quitting this position, I retain the second and third fingers in their places: the first finger, which held A only, takes four strings at the same fret where it is found, and by making the upper A with the fourth finger on the first string, I have under my fingers, not only the last two notes of that measure, but have also the hand placed for the whole of the measure following. In the other measure, there is but one part to be fingered, excepting in the last quarter. I finger this part according to the arrangement of the diatonic scale, by sliding the second finger from D to E, and the first from G sharp to A, in order to be able to make D sharp of the base with the second finger. I might explain this phrase again by the harmony; but I have promised not to employ any terms belonging to that science, with the exception of thirds and sixths, which are the keys to my whole fingering. In the following measure, I slide the little finger as far as C sharp, and the two notes E and C sharp being at the distance of a major sixth, which I should finger at the same fret, and consequently $^{4}_{3}$, if I were to make them with the fourth and second strings; but as, holding the fourth finger on the first string at the lower part of the fingerboard, I should seek for E and C sharp on the fifth and third strings, and these two strings open including a semitone more than the fourth and second, and than the third and first, I should employ for a major sixth the fingering which I should use on the others for a minor sixth, and I finger the first half of this measure $^{1}_{2}$. I observe that a major sixth D B commences the other half; but the B being preceded by the small note C sharp, and giving place to A sharp to return again, I do not finger the sixth $^{4}_{3}$, but $^{3}_{2}$, in order to manage with the first and second fingers for the other two notes. I slide the third finger on the first string to make E at the twelfth fret, and I ascend to take the minor sixth C sharp A, which begins the last measure of the symphony, and which prepares me for making the two thirds following.

After the commencement of the voice-part, the accompaniment is nearly like the symphony as far as to the last quarter of the sixth measure, plate XXIX, in which I consider the six semiquavers as only an exhibition of the parts separately, which form the chord at the pause. This chord offers me two minor thirds, B D, and G sharp B, and below them there are two E's octaves to each other. The two thirds employ four strings, and I have only two strings remaining for the two E's, consequently the higher of the two can be taken on the fifth string only. I take it with the first finger at the seventh fret, where, by barring, I find D and B forming a major sixth; and I want D G sharp, which form another. If I were not obliged to end with D, I should finger this sixth $^{3}_{4}$; but, the fourth finger being wanted for D, I finger the sixth, B G sharp, $^{3}_{2}$.

The fingering of the last three notes in the measure is obvious, as well as that of the first note of the measure following. I use the fourth finger on G in order to prepare myself for the fingering of the minor sixth, A F, $^{1}_{2}$. The third finger is found naturally on the base-note F, I pass it to the fifth string to make C, the only note that is not an open string in the last chord. This change is repeated in the following measure; but instead of passing the third finger back again from C to F, I remain on C and make F with the fourth. The first chord of the following measure contains a major sixth, F sharp D sharp, which I should finger $^{4}_{3}$, if C natural were not found between the two notes; but as I must make the C with the third finger, I finger the sixth $^{2}_{1}$. The second chord contains a minor sixth, G sharp E, and a minor third, B D, the sixths belonging to the sixth and fourth strings, which, when open, form a seventh, cannot have the same fingering as the sixths on strings tuned to a major sixth, I consequently finger this sixth $^{1}_{3}$, and the third $^{2}_{4}$.

The E, which I hold with the first finger, allows me to press the next two strings, at the same fret, to make A and C sharp. I quit this position to take advantage of the open first string for the E; and as the three following notes ascend by thirds, I finger the first $^{1}_{2}$, because it is major, and the little finger being already prepared for E, a minor third above C sharp, I have all that the measure contains. I see but two chords in the next: the first of these contains the major sixth, D B, which I should finger $^{3}_{4}$, but for the intervention of F sharp; this note is the major third above D, so that these three notes, having the same relation as the third, second, and first open strings, should be found at the same fret. I should take them with the first finger, if I had to make higher notes afterward; but the following chord being situated lower, I finger them $^{4}_{\substack{3\\2}}$, and reserve the first finger for taking the major sixth, B G sharp, of the following chord, to which I add E with the second finger on the second string, making $^{1}_{2}$ for the fingering of the major third, E G sharp. The fourth finger, on the fifth string, makes the base-note E. The following measure begins with a minor sixth, which I finger $^{1}_{2}$. Having to terminate the measure with the same sixth, and not having any other change before it than the major sixth, E C sharp, this E being a minor third above the other C sharp which I hold with the second finger, I take E and A at the same fret with the first finger, on the second and first strings, and instead of shifting the whole hand to finger this sixth $^{4}_{3}$, I extend the little finger to C sharp, finger it $^{4}_{1}$, and have only to raise the little finger to have again C sharp A $^{1}_{2}$. With the fingering $^{4}_{3}$ on the third and second strings, I make the third, D F sharp, commencing the other measure, and I make on the fourth and second strings the sixth, found in the second chord, the first finger readily stopping the base on the fifth string at the seventh fret. By this fingering, I find myself at the proper place for producing the minor sixth, which begins the following measure; and, by taking A on the first string, I also press the second, which produces E. An extension of the little finger gives me the first of the three notes, which complete the upper part of this measure; and the reader ought to perceive, that the third, made by the second and first fingers, is the foundation of this position. I begin the next measure by sliding the first finger from A to G sharp; I do not however slide the hand, but must retain it in position, to make the major sixth, D B, $^{4}_{3}$, for which the fourth finger should be placed from the commencement, that it may be struck with the open string B. It is only at B of the upper part, that I quit this position to take up another at the twelfth fret on the second string, which enables me to play all the phrase near E, beginning the following measure; descending by thirds, and the first being minor, the fingering $^{1}_{4}$ will make it without displacing the hand, as well as the A on the second string with the second finger. The third finger falls naturally on the fourth string at the eleventh fret, and with the second I finger the minor sixth, C sharp A. The upper part of the four following measures, proceeding gradually towards E, on the first string at the twelfth fret, I avoid the high part of the fingerboard, that I may find myself less distant from the object in view, and the figures will show the reader the method which I constantly employ with the assistance of the fingering of the thirds and sixths.

By analysing all the phrases of this accompaniment, I should be obliged to repeat myself too frequently, and the reader's attention would be fatigued in vain. What I have written thus far ought to convince him that the knowledge and practice of thirds and sixths constitute the whole secret of my play; and I shall therefore explain in a few places only hereafter.

The second measure of plate XXXII is nothing but a chord (with its notes separated for the right hand), the position of which is founded on the minor sixth, $^{2}_{3}$, G E flat, which places the first finger where it bars five strings, among which are comprised C and G. The little finger presses the third string by the side of the fourth, and produces me the C which is found between G and E. By this means I avoid all motion of the left hand, and the sounds have more resonance. It is for this reason that I finger the following measure as pointed out by the figures.

In the fifth measure of plate XXXIII, as soon as the descending semitones have made me employ the first finger, I bring it down by diatonic degrees to have it on B, which is the minor sixth of D sharp, the fingering of which $^{3}_{2}$ enables me to finish the phrase without deranging the hand. In the sixth measure, I find it easier to slide the second finger from C sharp to C natural, leaving time for the first finger to prepare itself for D sharp, than to employ it for C natural, and make it pass suddenly to D sharp. For the same reason, I cause the second finger to slide on three notes in the fifth measure of plate XXXVI; but as the G sharp in the following measure is found an octave higher than the preceding G sharp, I finger the passage differently.

For the rest, I may simplify this analysis by mentioning the basis of the fingering of every position. In the fourth measure, plate XXXVIII, the sixth, C sharp A. In the sixth measure, although I observe the sixth, G sharp E, therein, I take advantage of the first and second strings open. In the seventh of Plate XXXVIII, I keep the same position, because it is the same chord produced by the same notes.

In the eighth, I again meet with the third C sharp E, and the sixth, C sharp A.

In the first of Plate XXXIX, the major third, D F sharp, and minor third, F sharp A.

In the second, the minor sixth, C sharp A, and major sixth, B G sharp.

In the third, the minor sixth, C sharp A, and afterward it is a repetition of the sixth measure, plate XXXV, as far as to the last measure of plate XXXIX, where the foundation of the position is the third, B D, or the minor sixth, B G, which I bar in order to take the base-note G, with the same finger. In the first measure of Plate XL, the third, B D, having become major by the sharp before D, the fingering $^{3}_{2}$ guides my position.

In the second it is still the minor sixth, C sharp A, which occupies half the third measure, and the other half is the major sixth, D B.

The fourth measure of plate XL is again founded on the minor sixth, C sharp A, to the last quarter, which is a major third, A C sharp, of which the fingering serves me as a guide and point of support for three quarters of the fifth measure. The last quarter of this measure contains the major sixth, D B. The sixth measure is like the second The first quarter of the seventh measure is the result of the fingering of the preceding measure; the second quarter is the major sixth, E C sharp, or the major third, A C sharp; and the last, the minor third, G sharp B, or the major sixth, D B, which I bar, in order to make the E, which is found at the same fret. The first chord of the eighth measure contains the minor sixth, C sharp A, and the major third, A C sharp. The second chord is founded on the major sixth, B G sharp, made on the fourth and second strings; the first chord of the ninth measure, on the major third, A C sharp, which the necessity of making A on the fourth string at the seventh fret obliges me to finger $^{3}_{4}$. The second chord has for the basis of the fingering the major sixth, B G sharp, made on the fourth and second strings, with its proper fingering, $^{3}_{4}$.

The final chord is the first of the seventh measure.

I think I have completely proved that the knowledge of the thirds and sixths is the foundation of the whole fingering in regard to harmony. I shall not cease exhorting those who would devote themselves to the study of the guitar, to endeavour to acquire this knowledge. A guitarist, who is a harmonist, will always have an advantage over one who is not. Even a tolerable player on the pianoforte (the first of instruments to produce harmony), has already acquired very useful musical habits in regard to the guitar.* A tolerable pianist cannot be a bad guitarist. A few years ago, I

---

* Besides the young lady mentioned in the introduction, I have recently had a proof of what I have just said, in the rapid progress of Miss Mary Jane Burdett, (daughter of Mr Arthur Burdett,) a young lady who plays well on the pianoforte. Engaged in completing her education, she devotes herself to several kinds of study at once, as well the necessary as the agreeable, and consequently cannot give up her time exclusively to the study of the guitar. My principles, and the direction which her ideas have taken, from being habituated to the progression and contexture of pianoforte-music, have enabled her, in twenty-eight lessons, to play my *Fantaisie*, opera 40, which I have dedicated to her,—a result which I have never been able to obtain in so few lessons from other pupils, who did not play on the pianoforte, and who, with the best inclination, devoted themselves exclusively to the study of the guitar. It is true, they had previously acquired habits which prevented a free style of playing, and, unfortunately, they had been taught to perceive only notes, where it was necessary to see music.

saw some works for the guitar, written by an author whose talents enjoyed a certain degree of reputation. In these I discerned the man whose musical education had been acquired on an instrument of melody. In other works which I have seen I found sufficient regularity in the progression of the base; when the parts of the harmony are incomplete, the author almost always suppresses the part which ought in preference to be omitted: in short, I observed in them a plan and management. The reason of this is because the author plays on the pianoforte, and it is to the habits acquired by the execution of the music for that instrument, that he owes the reputation he so justly enjoys Never having heard him myself, I speak without hesitation after the testimony of persons whose opinion I consider of great weight.

"You require then," I shall be asked, "that a guitarist must be a harmonist? Again I say, that I require nothing at all; but it would be desirable he should be so, since the guitar is an instrument of harmony. "But so is the pianoforte to a much greater degree: the music performed on it is much more complicated than guitar-music; and yet it is not necessary to be a harmonist in order to play on it." The music given to be studied on the pianoforte, simple and easy as it may be, is written correctly, almost always well composed, and the pupil acquires a habit of correctness, of a regular progression of the base, natural transitions, chords well prepared and properly resolved; but unfortunately all guitar-music is not of this kind. Generally the easiest is the least correct, because it has been agreed to call correctness difficulty. It is this music which forms the ideas of learners, and consequently has given occasion to connoisseurs, on hearing a poor, faulty, monotonous, and insignificant orchestral accompaniment, to call it a *guitar accompaniment.* Let the easiest works for the guitar be correct; let a pupil who is learning a piece in two parts only feel their progression, distinguishing in his mind the one from the other; then I believe that he may, without being a harmonist, play well. A child, without any natural defect of organisation, acquires the pronunciation, and even the manner of speaking, of the persons who converse with him continually. This is no hypothesis, but an indisputable fact. Give him, for a few years, a preceptor whose pronunciation is defective, and let him in earnest take his teacher as a pattern, he will believe the pronunciation to be proper, and will pronounce the same. If later in life he may wish to correct himself, supposing he may succeed, it will only be with much labour and trouble.

Yet I think the day will come when learners of the guitar will form their ideas by correct music. I am not the only one that writes such music. Still more would be met with, but for that insuperable reason—*an author mnst live!* When I arrived in France, people said to me, "Make us some easy tunes:" I was very willing to do so; but I discovered that *easy* meant *incorrect*, or, at least, *incomplete.* A very celebrated guitarist told me that he had been obliged to give up writing in my manner, because the editors had openly declared to him, "It is one thing to appreciate compositions as a connoisseur, and another as a music-seller: it is necessary to write silly trifles for the public. I like your work, but it would not return me the expenses of printing." What was to be done? *An author must live!* And he composed works from which I never could have guessed his merit, if I had not had other means of forming a better opinion of him. Others, who are very far from being comparable with him, will write some trifle that can be played in three lessons; and the scholar's self-love is interested in thinking it pretty. His master will make a present of it to a publisher, provided he is allowed a score of copies, for *he must make himself known.* He performs it in parties, is applauded, and presents a copy to the lady, whose acquaintance he imagines can procure him pupils. The publisher, on his side, is interested in over-praising it, to cover the expenses of printing: he is an excellent composer as to sale; and then he teaches very well, for he has enabled a pupil in three lessons to play the piece which he performs himself. Pupils increase in number, and he takes good care not to make them acquainted with any other music than his own, or than music of a similar nature. He is a teacher and must also be an author. He will take a known fashionable air, employ it as a subject with a base made by the open strings, or a few notes made with the thumb above the fingerboard; the theme divided into notes of half the original value, will be the first variation, into triplets the second. He will make a piece of the same number of measures as the the theme, and call it the *minore,* because it will indeed be in the minor mode, in which he will introduce a great many *coulcs* and *glisses* (slides or glidings*), that the execution may produce a more expressive and touching effect. This minore is to be played somewhat slowly, the better to contrast with the grand arpeggios in the major mode, reserved for the most showy part of the following variations, which, if desired, may be the last. He is now an author, and must write a Method: nothing is easier. It is but to copy a few elements of solfeggio—the A B C, and include in six pages what everybody knows—the value and names of the notes, to write fingered scales in the keys he may have practiced, † a few passages or arpeggios, which he will adorn with the title of *Exercises*, and especially a great many *airs*.

Instead of *studying* the method of M. Carulli, he will mutilate the text of it ‡ by making an extract, in order that his work, being less voluminous, may be reputed more simple, and that a publisher may make fewer difficulties in purchasing it. *An author must live!* If any one makes observations to him on his work, he will take good care not to pay attention to them, nor to discuss the subject. His whole reply will be, "Every one has his own way;" but the cue is, "An author must live!" A learner will say to him, "I have heard Mr. N. He played a fantasia on the air N—Ah! what a pretty piece! I should like to have it; is it published? Should I be able to make it out?" Then the answer is quite ready—"Oh! certainly, it must be an excellent piece. He has wonderful talent! but that exceeds all limits; it is a different style; § and it is rashness to pretend to play his music. He writes for himself alone, there are continual barred notes and deviations, it is no longer within the fingering or powers of the instrument. He writes that for the pianoforte, and indeed I do not believe that he plays all that he writes: there are a great many notes merely for the eye. However it is a pity that *he does not give lessons*, for he would either tell us how to play them, or we should see what notes he omits in performance. But, is it a wonder? All great talents have a spice of folly. He no longer cares about the guitar. He has a whim for writing for the orchestra, and a mania for travelling, which occasions him to remain but for three or four months in a place." If the spirit of that reply is, "A man must live," I do not think that he generalises: "I must live" would perhaps be more significant. But this must terminate: those who write properly prove that it is possible to be both easy and correct. Their works will become the only ones that

---

* I believe it is thus that the action is called of passing one finger for the whole length of the finger-board, along a string played at the point of departure, so that all the semitones are heard, giving the music a peculiar grace, and repose to the performer. If I mistake the meaning of the word, I beg a little indulgence in favour of the sincerity with which I confess my ignorance of an article too important for me to run the risk of leading into error the reader who should kindly believe me on my word.

† He will attribute to the instrument the difficulty that he will experience in the other keys.

‡ It should be said to him who employs this procedure, "Endeavour first to play like him, and when you shall have acquired his skill, you will be allowed to reason on the necessity which you appear to suppose of a change or simplification in his system of teaching."

§ This expression leads me, perhaps, beyond the bounds which I had laid down for myself. *A different style!* Is it possible that beings of this class can imagine that their own is one! I have always thought that style was the application of fundamental principles, on which two artists are agreed, to different objects. I see that the style of Piron was not that of Racine, but they were both poets, they were agreed on the qualities requisite in a sonnet, an elegy, an ode, &c.; and it might have been said of one, without offending the other, that he had a *different style*. Potier, Talma, and Odry, were three true actors. Hogarth and Raphael had the same principles of design and of optics, and their productions, though in different styles, prove that they were in accord as to the truths of that art. But what shall we say of him who, having never reasoned on the proportions of the human body, and without any other principles of drawing than a habit acquired, by dint of practice, of placing nearly right the outline of a figure, should have the impudence to exhibit one of his paintings, and, when spoken to about the Guido of Guerino, should reply, "It is in another style?" Guerino would laugh at it, because he knows that the public would do the same; but, unfortunately, the public are not so clear-sighted in music as in painting; and "it is in another style" is more frequently pronounced than I should have thought, among an illustrious people. Ignorance and knavery have combined to mislead them, and I am surprised at the success of their undertaking. For my own part, I could not help saying: "As long as you design for yourself alone, or for those whose judgment is in relation with yours, do what you please, nobody has anything to say against it; but if you would expose your productions to the public, consult connoisseurs to ascertain beforehand if they are worthy of it; and, especially, if you compose a didactic work on the art in which you think yourself learned, be certain that you know what you engage to speak of. Respect the public, and do not render them the dupes of your ignorance. If you are obliged to teach, follow one of the methods that proves the author to have reasoned well: your modesty will make you play a much more honourable part than that which you prepare for yourself by the foolish vanity of pretending to have *created a style*.

will form scholars. I know some that are extremely useful,* but the manner in which they are considered, by some persons, destroys all advantages that might be derived from them : † this is not the fault of the author.

ON FINGERING WITH THE RING-FINGER.

I promised on page 20, to speak of the employment of the fourth finger of the right hand ; ‡ and although in the piece, the accompaniment to which I have just analysed, it should be employed in certain chords, I have previously said nothing respecting it. My motive was, that, in the article *Right Hand,* stated on page 11, what was the case wherein I used it ; and, as in the accompaniment in question, it is not employed otherwise, I thought it useless to return to the subject. In this place I should remark that, in a succession of chords, the upper part of which forms a melody which ought to predominate, as the finger, which is to produce it, is weaker than the others, I curve it more in the act of touching the string ; for being shorter than the medius it cannot encounter the string so far from the bridge ; and it impels it at a point offering greater resistance than the deep strings offer to the other fingers. I have therefore found it necessary to make it acquire by its curvature the power refused to it by nature, as well from the construction of the bones of the hand as from the derivation of the nerves by which they are actuated. §

In the 85th example, Plate XLI, the upper notes form a melody requiring the employment of the fourth (third) finger in the manner indicated ; but when the upper note is not accompanied by three others, I never use more than three fingers (the thumb and two fingers). The weakness and the difference in length of the medius and ring-finger (the second and third) render it incumbent on me to be sparing in the use of the latter. By using it, I depart in some degree from the principle which I have laid down, namely, to keep the hand quiet, and avoid the action of pulling up the strings. I not only remove the finger a little, but I give it another motion, that the object of this removal may be attained only in regard to the string played by the finger in question. This motion consists in turning the hand a little in a direction contrary to that in which I observe it turned by some guitarists. Instead of separating it on the side of the thumb, I separate it on the side of the little finger, so that the extremity of the medius (or second) being considered as the centre of this motion, the thumb and fore-finger approaching the strings as much as the ring-finger (third) and little finger remove from them, this approximation compensates for the removal of the hand ; and hence my three principal fingers remain in their places.

CONCLUSION.

I never could conceive how a Method could be made with a much greater quantity of examples than of text. In half a page of writing all the rules of grammar are employed, and a volume scarcely contains them. I have seen Methods for singing, the text of which was reduced to teaching the names of what was to be done, such as *volata*, *appoggiatura*, *grupetto*, *mordente*, *mesa di voce*, *portamento*, *trillo*, &c., presenting afterwards gradually all the results to be produced and the difficulties to be overcome ; so that it contained *what was to be sung :* ‖ but I have never seen a

---

* Certain Duos by Carulli are of the number.

† They think that, by having the fingering marked, they are acquainted with the method.

‡ In every other case I should call this the *third* finger, to employ the same nomenclature as for the left hand. (Foreigners generally reckon the thumb as the first finger, our first as the second, &c.—Tr.)

§ Examine the ramifications of the nerves of the arm, the arrangement of the bones of the hand, and the cause will be found of the weakness and stiffness of the ring-finger, as well as my reason for holding the thumb of the left hand opposite the medius, or second finger.

‖ I compare those who teach in this way to quack doctors, whom they ridicule, perhaps, without perceiving that to prescribe a medicine according to this or that symptom, without understanding anatomy or chemistry, and consequently in total ignorance of the nature of the simples whose mixture they prescribe, of their mode of action, and of the process by which they are to produce in the animal economy the intended effect, is exactly the same thing as to make scales, swell and diminish sounds, &c. without having previously questioned nature as to the way of producing, changing, and modifying those sounds to make use of which they are to teach, only *quia ita voluerunt priora.* Reason with them, and they will become angry, or turn your reasoning into ridicule. *Mio Maestro faceva così,* is their shield ; and if they avoid discussion on the subject, it is because their pretended principles are all derived from practice, and not in any degree from analysis, or from reasoning on observations.

I have not contented myself with what experience has taught me,—that all my fingers have not the same power nor freedom of motion. I have consulted a treatise on anatomy and a skeleton to know the cause ; and it was after obtaining that knowledge that I established my principles.

single Method wherein the author, having consulted the action of the lungs and the conformation of our organ, as well as the process by which it modifies the column of air to which it offers a passage, tells me how I ought to proceed to perform with less trouble what I see written; for, in fine, nature must have a procedure answering to what we call *fingering* on instruments. Man has wrung from her the secret of the planetary motions; and because a celebrated philosopher has said that the speaking voice is the result of a process different from that of the singing voice, I must stop here, and call idle talk the reasons founded on a knowledge of the organs. It was probably from this cause that a singing master said to me (apparently thinking to say something clever), "You should advise students of surgery first to learn music, since you would have a singing master learn anatomy." I am of opinion that, when the matter in question is to methodize an action, it is essential to know the agents of it in order to establish rules for the purpose of employing them in the manner most analagous to their functions. Musical examples tell me clearly enough what I am to do; but the text should tell me how I am to do it, and should teach me all the ways of employing my powers, make them known to me, make me sensible that he who prescribes rules speaks advisedly—with knowledge of the subject, and that these rules are the fruit of his conviction and not of his belief. Blind submission of the reason degrades the human mind, when it occurs in other instances than those of religious faith. But, I shall be told, experience is a great master. Yes, when we reason on what we perceive; but when facts only serve to fill the memory, presumption occasions a worse progress than feeling in the dark, for it inspires rashness when it is necessary to have caution and prudence.

I have supposed that he who buys a Method means to learn it. I have thought it my duty to make him acquainted with all my reasons for establishing the fundamental principles of mine. He who desires to have only a collection of numerous progressive airs, will do wrong to purchase a work which I never should allow myself to use as a means of selling productions which I could or could not dispose of otherwise. For the explanation of a theory or the application of a rule, it is unnecessary to multiply examples: a single example is sufficient, if well explained. An author should give his work an appropriate title: *method, exercises, lessons*, and *studies* are by no means synonimous *

If, in the explanation which I have just given, the reader finds me too diffuse, he should forgive it on account of the rectitude of my intention. I might, under shelter of the opinion with which Europe has kindly honoured my name, have indicated rules superficially, and made a great volume of music, wherein had been found a collection of arpeggio passages, under the name of exercises, a collection of waltz and dance-tunes, a great many romances, all with nearly the same accompaniments. I should have avoided whatever requires reflection, and I think too that I should have found, as well as another, means to dazzle the learner who should have desired to study my method, by enabling him immediately to play pieces which would induce him to believe that he had learnt something, whilst I should only have prevented his becoming acquainted with the instrument, by the false manner in which I had caused him to study it. I have never lost sight of the true meaning of the word *Method*. If several singing masters call method that which I call *style*, and if they call style *taste*, that is no ground for my giving the lie to the dictionary in their favour; nor for my reasoning at present otherwise than I did at the time when I digested the thoughts which I have communicated to the reader. He who wishes to follow me will find that the object of my theories is to teach and persuade, since I establish nothing by authority. These are not precepts which I give, but researches which I communicate. Those persons whose study and practice have been directed away from what is more simple and natural, say that my guitar-music is extremely difficult, without perceiving that all the secret of my playing consists in two scales in use with all guitarists.

---

* *Method*, a Treatise on the established principles on which the rules are founded, which ought to guide the operations.

Exercises, pieces of music, each having for its object to make us familiar with the application of the rules. Exercises are the practice of theories established by the method (which I consider as the speculative part), as the use of the square for raising a perpendicular is the result of a certain geometrical demonstration.

Lessons, pieces of music, each having for its object not the exercise of a single rule merely, but also of the rules employed in the lessons preceding, and even the initiating of the learner in some exceptions.

Studies, exercises on exceptions, and on rules offering greater difficulties in their application.

It is true that they have studied to render them difficult, by fingering them in a manner directly opposed to that which the construction of the hand indicates by the different lengths of the fingers. Do I then write what is difficult, or is it the rooted habit of proceeding in a contrary direction which occasions it to be difficult to proceed straight forward? If I keep constantly in a half-darkened room only for a month, the first time I shall afterward see moderate daylight I shall find it too strong, but shall not say so. I shall say it produces that effect upon me, because my eyes have lost the habit of seeing the full quantity of light which nature has enabled them to support; and if I find any fault, it will not be with daylight, but with him by whom I was induced to renounce the free exercise of my visual faculty; and still much more, if in the commencement I had had a great deal of trouble in doing so. What beginner does not suffer exceedingly in the wrist, if the master makes him support the guitar in the way represented by figure 12, page 12? Is there anything more common than to hear it said, "I have practised very hard to-day; I have broken my wrist and have blisters on all my fingers, and particularly at the root of my fore-finger."

I conceive that music, written to be fingered by the fingers at full length, must be difficult with fingers shortened one half; but is it one of the commandments to hold one half of the hand behind the neck? Are we not often obliged to break that commandment, if it be one? How else can the 86th example be performed? "But you give us church music and counterpoint. Give us guitar-music. Come out from your strong-hold. Speak to us in the language most in use." I will do so most willingly.

Even when the thumb is used for G in the base commenceing the 87th example, plate XLI, and it is made with the second finger (or more probably with the third), a player cannot do otherwise than place the hand in my manner for the second half measure, and particularly for the first chord of the second half. All those who play on the guitar do the same, because there is no other way; but phrases constructed entirely in the manner of that example are not found in my compositions, and it is admitted, that it is my name only that will give it the stamp of difficulty, because it has been thought proper to call the position, which appears to me to be the most natural, a *deviation*, and to call the contraction of the muscles and tendons the natural position. Shall I be in the right in saying that the handle of a fork is too short, and that it is very difficult to use it, because instead of raising the arm to carry it to the mouth, I choose to stoop my head down to my hand? Where is then that great difficulty attributed to my works?

My Duo, in the major key of A, *Les Deux Amis*, is extremely easy in comparison with the works of other amateurs, who have the reputation of writing easy music. The part of Mr. Aguado only has a very rapid variation, but it is in single notes and in the style most known.* My part is the least complicated of what I have hitherto done. My object was to produce the best effect at the smallest expense.

My twenty-four exercises are the easiest that can be written in that style. I allow that, in my twenty-four lessons, I had not sufficient patience, and that the difference from one to another is too striking: it was necessary to give the learner as much attention as the music; but, after having learnt the exercises, these lessons become in consequence easier.

I have now explained all that constitutes the Method which I wrote for myself. It is the result of many years of observation and reflection. I made mistakes, and have been indebted to them for a multitude of reflections which I never should have made perhaps without the necessity of self-correction: so true it is that, when we reason, we can derive advantage from the involuntary errors we may have committed. I request the reader to examine well my reasons, and not to sanction them without judging of their validity. I may deceive myself, being no more exempt from error than another person; but I am for plain dealing, and, because I endeavour to prove what I advance, I can never admit a contrary opinion but by virtue of sufficient reasons. A smart saying, raillery, quoting an authority, will not amount to proof, and I have a right to require a just reciprocity.

---

* Before playing Hummel's Trio on the *Sentinelle* with Messrs. Herz and Lafont, I was obliged to make the guitar-variation, example 88, plate XLII; because the one found in the trio presented much greater difficulties than mine. After this confession it may be seen, that, if the *peculiar* style of the guitar is that of the variation in question, I am not so skilful on that instrument as the writer. I could perform it; but it would be at the expense of principles from which I could never willingly depart.

I shall conclude this explanation by a summary of general maxims, which I observe, as the result of all that has been said.—

First.—To regard the effect of the music more than the praise as to skill as a performer.

Second.—To require more from *skill* than from *strength.*

Third.—To be sparing of the operations called barring and shifting.

Fourth.—To consider fingering as an art, having for its object to make me find the notes I want, within reach of the fingers that are to produce them, without the continual necessity of making deviations for the purpose of seeking them.

Fifth.—Never to make any ostentation of difficulty in my playing, for by doing so, I should render difficult what is the least so.

Sixth.—Never to give work to the weakest fingers, whilst the strongest are doing nothing.

Seventh.—Not to fall into a too common error, which proceeds from very accurate reasoning in regard to the pianoforte, but is very ill applied to the guitar, namely, not to hold a finger down longer than the duration of the note which it is to produce. As long as the finger presses down the key of the pianoforte, it allows the wires to continue in vibration, and the sound, blending with that of another key, would produce an effect incompatible with purity of performance; but two or three consecutive notes being made on the same string of the guitar, if their progression be ascending, the second damps and terminates the sound of the first, and the third that of the second. If by letting fall the finger which makes the second, I at the same time raise the finger which stopped the first, I make two actions instead of one, and even run the risk of raising the finger a moment too soon, and making the open string sound, which, instead of rendering my performance purer, would give it less purity. If the notes are descending, instead of waiting for the moment in which the note ought to be produced, to press the string, I have the finger already upon it, and have no other action to perform than that of raising the finger which stopped the highest note. This again spares me one motion, and besides a display which I have never approved.

Eighth.—To avoid a lateral motion which some guitarists think graceful, namely, to leave the parallel direction between the line formed by the ends of the fingers and the line of the strings. For example, in the successive notes A (on the first string), G, F sharp, E, D (on the second string), on making A they have the ends of the fingers in an excellent direction; but as soon as the little finger quits A, it goes off the finger-board, G quits it in turn; and when the first finger remains alone on F sharp, the line of the ends of the fingers makes an angle of 45 degrees with the string, or rather all the hand is removed behind the neck, because they have made the wrist do that which, being done by the fingers, would give facility to the second to make D on the second string, without the wrist's being obliged to make a motion to replace the hand before the neck, unless the D be produced with the flat finger, which requires much more force, and I know not how it could be done without pressing the first string also on G, when, perhaps, I should want it as an open string immediately, and I should be obliged to make a motion again to leave it at liberty. When my hand is in a position, and the passage does not form harmony, I place the wrist so that a straight line drawn from the first finger to the fourth shall be parallel to the string. I hold the wrist motionless, and keep my fingers over the place where they are to act.

Ninth.—When it is a question of a great distance in the width of the finger-board, and the little finger holds one of the extremities, to take the other extremity with the longest finger.

Tenth.—When a difficulty of position occurs, to consult the least inconvenient situation for the weakest finger, and to lay the task on the stronger.

Eleventh.—When it is necessary to give to the line of the ends of the fingers a direction parallel to the fret instead of the string, to make this change depend rather on the position of the elbow than on the motion of the wrist.

Twelfth and last.—To hold reasoning for a great deal, and routine for nothing.

FINIS.

CIRENCESTER: PRINTED BY WILLIAM FOWLER.

Ex: 1.
Ex: 2.
Ex: 3.
Ex: 4.
Ex: 5.
Ex: 6.
Ex: 7.
Ex: 8.
Ex: 9.
Ex: 10
Ex: 11.
6th String in D.
Ex: 12
Ex: 13.
Andante Largo.
Ex: 14.
Fine.

Open Strings.

Ex: 15.

ARRANGEMENT OF THE MAJOR DIATONIC SCALE.

Ex: 16. Notes.

SCALE.

Ex: 17.

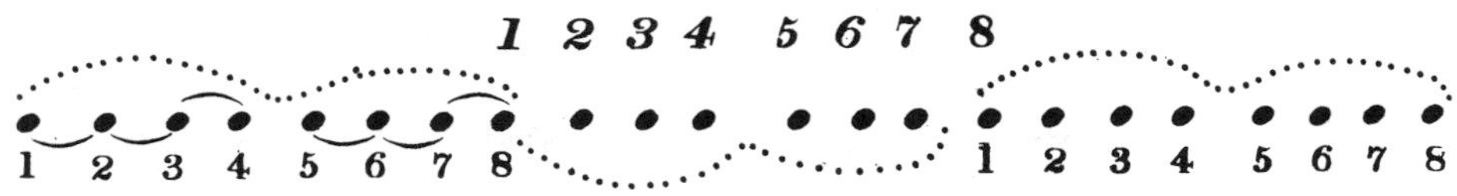

Ex: 18.

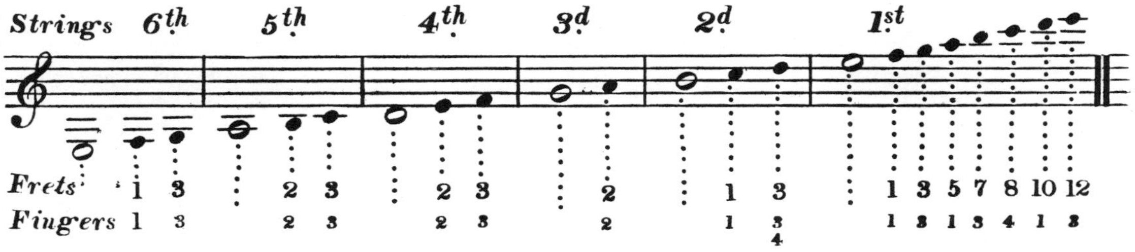

SIXTH STRING.

Ex: 19.

FIFTH STRING.

IV

FOURTH STRING.

THIRD STRING.

SECOND STRING.

Tonic
2d
3d
4th
5th
6th
7th
Ex: 20
Right Hand.
Ex: 21.
Ex: 22
1
2
3
4
5
6
Ex: 23

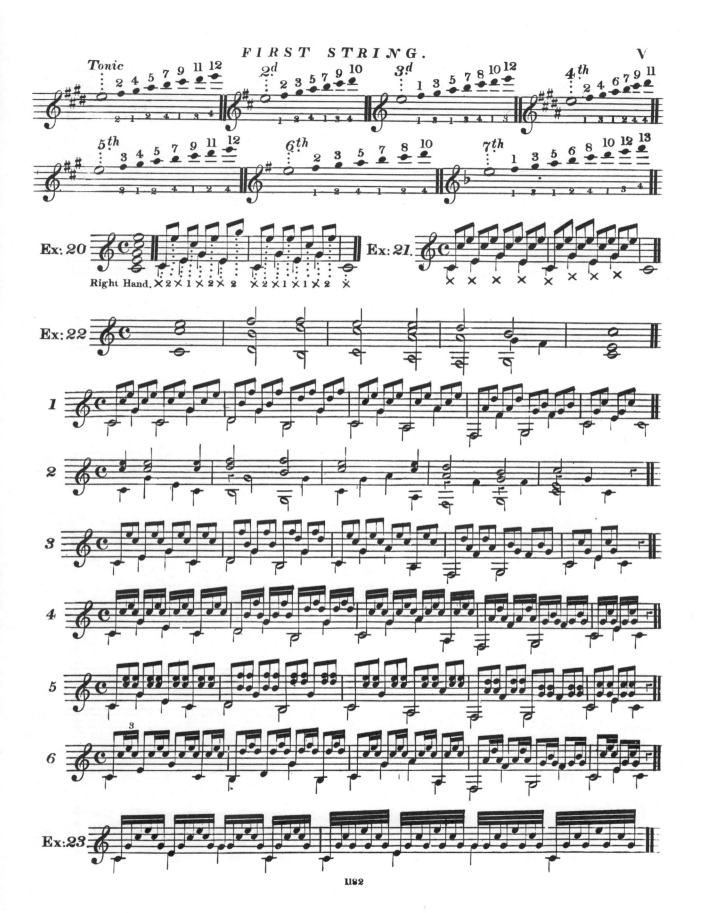

Ex: 24.

Ex: 25.

Ex: 26.

Ex: 27.
ff
ff
&c
Ex: 28.
Ex: 29.
Ex: 30.
Right Hand.
Ex: 31.

Ex: 33.

FORMULA FOR THIRDS.

	1st Semitone	1. Tone.	1. Tone.	1. Tone.	1.½ Tone.	1. Tone.	1. Tone.	1.
Fingers:	2d Tone.	3. Tone.	3.½ Tone.	2. Tone.	2. Tone.	3. Tone.	3.½ Tone.	2.
Thirds:	Major	Minor	Minor	Major	Major	Minor	Minor	Major

Ex: 34.

Ex: 35.

Ex: 36.

Ex: 37.

Ex: 38.

X
Ex: 39.
Ex: 40.
Ex: 41.
Ex: 42
Ex: 43.
ON SIXTHS.
Ex: 44.
Ex: 45.
Major.
Major.
Minor.
Ex: 46.
Major.
Major.
Minor.
Minor.
Ex: 47.
Ex: 48.

EXERCISES ON THIRDS.

XII

EXERCISES ON SIXTHS.

XIV

5.

6.

EXERCISES ON THIRDS AND SIXTHS

Ex: 49.
Ex: 50.
Fingers
Strings
4th
3d
2d
1st
Ex: 51.
4th
3d
2d
1st
Ex: 52.
4th
3d
2d
1st
Ex: 53.
4th
3d
2d
1st
5th
4th
3d
2d
1st
Ex: 54.
4th
3d
2d
1st
Ex: 55.
4th
3d
2d
1st
Ex: 56.
4th
3d
2d
1st
3d
2d

Ex: 57.

Ex: 58.

Ex: 59.

Ex: 60.

Ex: 61.

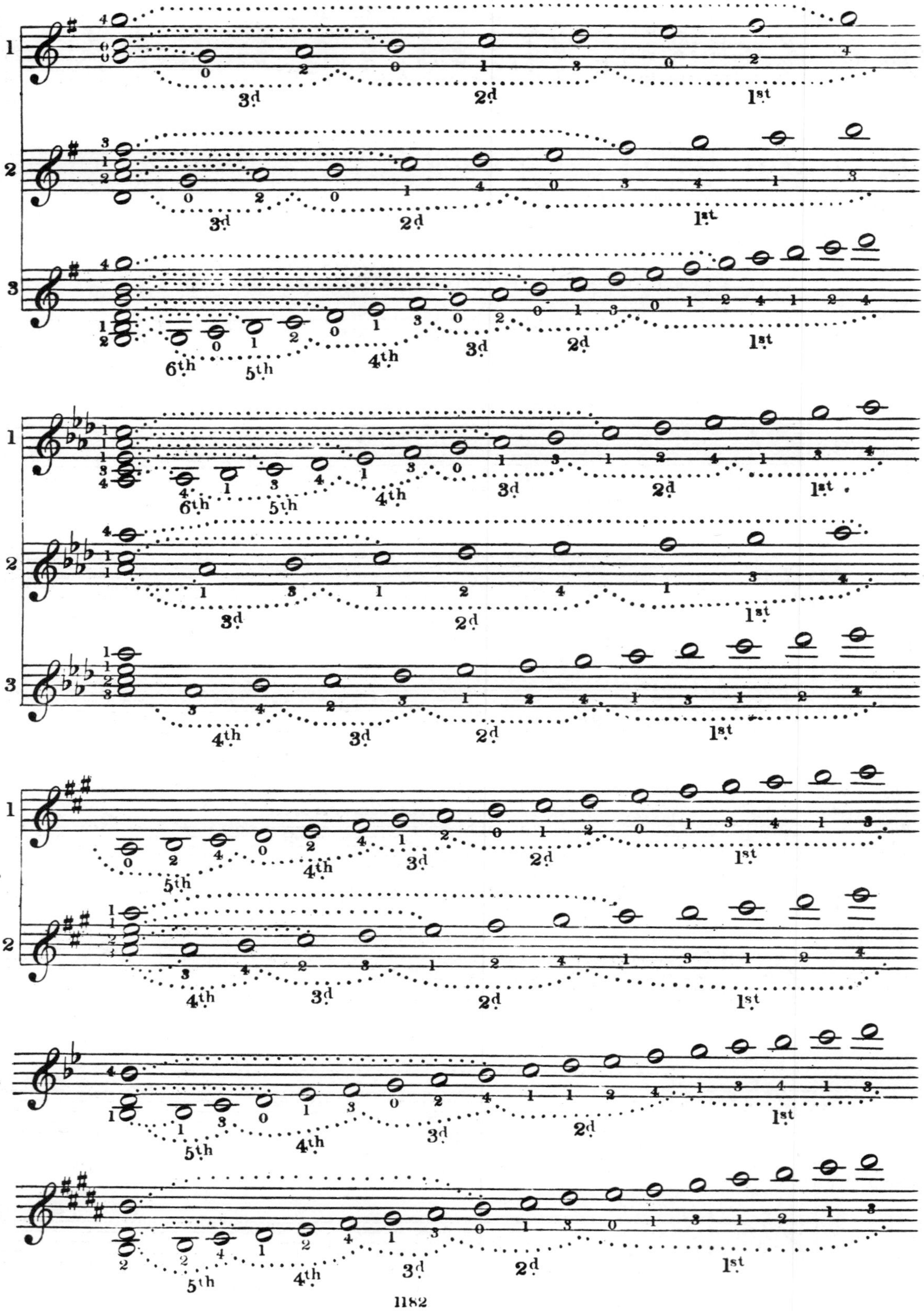

Ex: 62.

Ex: 63.

Ex: 64.

Ex: 65.
Ex: 66.
Ex: 67.
Ex: 68.
Ex: 69.
Ex: 70.
Chord.
Chord.
Chord.
Ex: 71.
Tonic or Key-Note
D
Ex: 72.
2d
3d
4th
5th
6th
7th

Ex: 73.

Ex: 74.

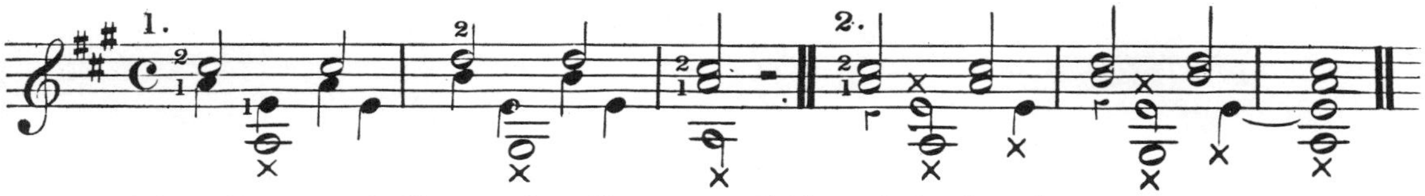

The figures indicate the fingers of the right hand.

A TABLE OF HARMONIC SOUNDS.

Ex: 75.

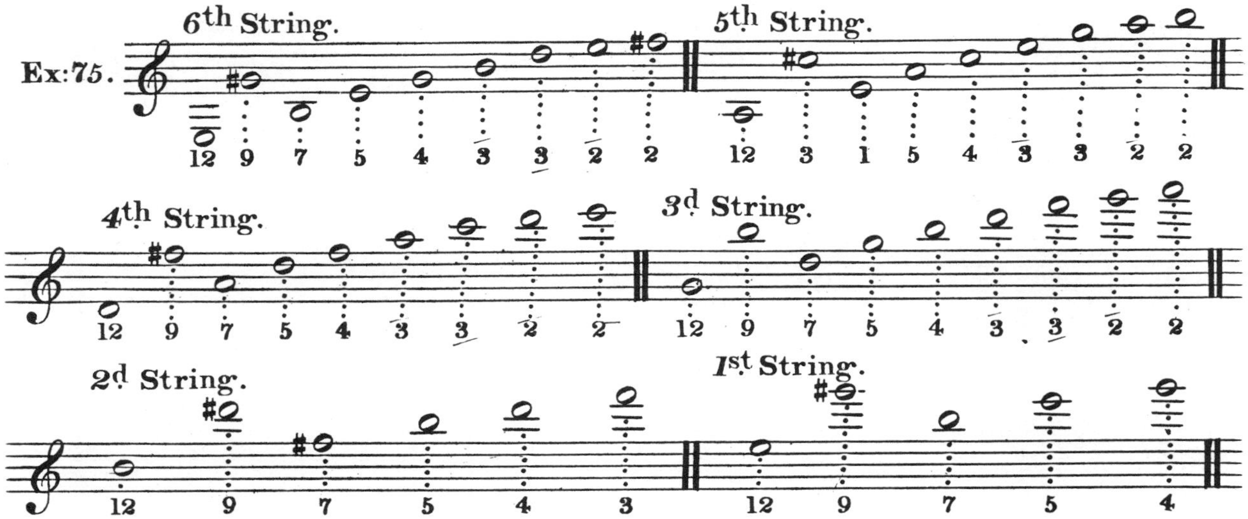

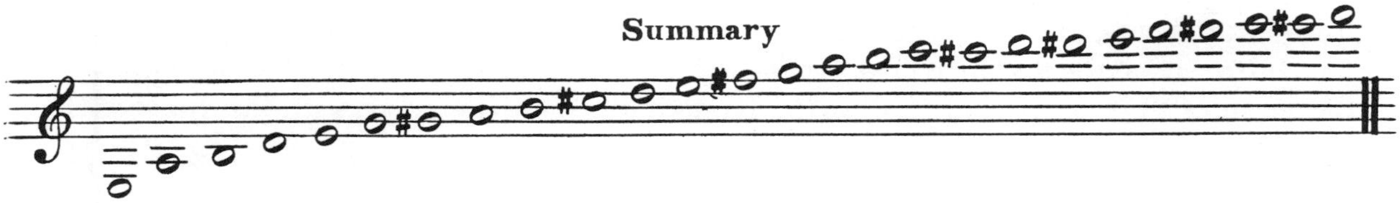

Ex: 76.

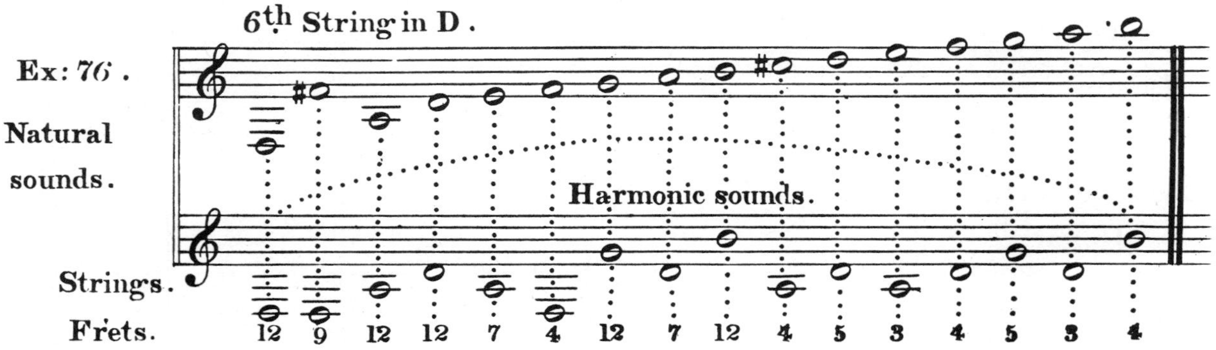

Ex: 77. 6th String in F.

Natural sounds.

Strings.

Frets.

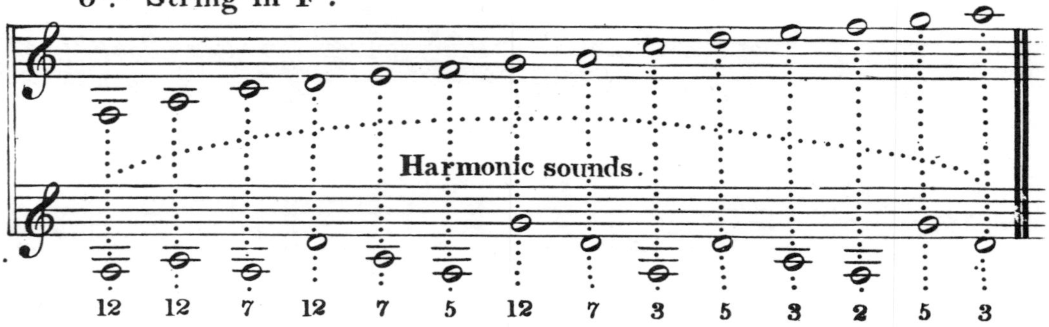

RELATION OF THE TWO CLEFS.

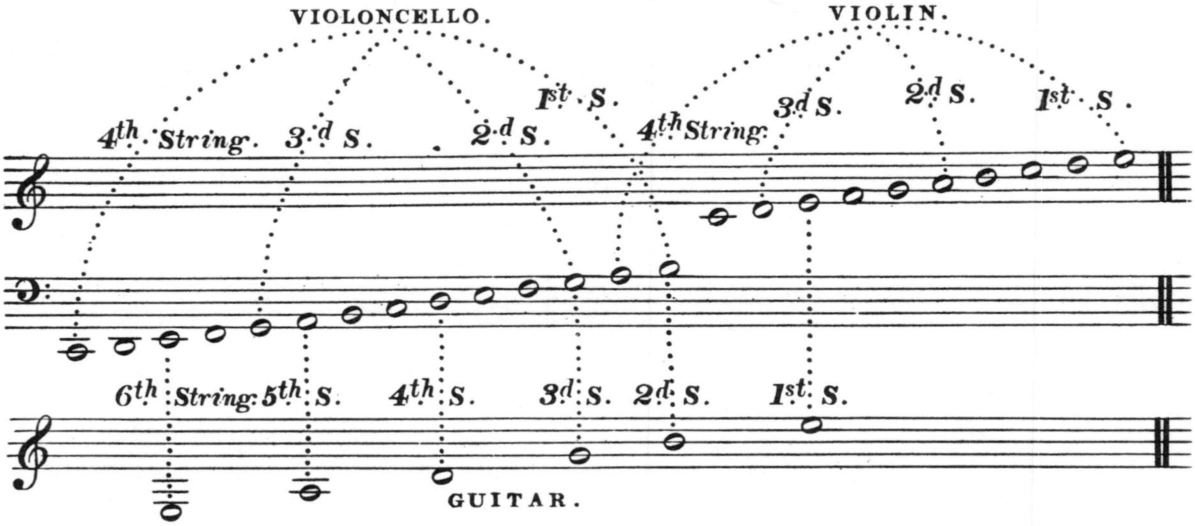

By examining the length and diameter of the strings and comparing the sizes of these three instruments, I think it will be obvious why the first string of the Violin and the first of the Guitar are at the distance of an octave and the fourth string of the Guitar in unison with the second of the Violoncello, as well as the fourth of the Violin in unison with the third of the Guitar.

Harmonic sounds.

True Scale of the Guitar.

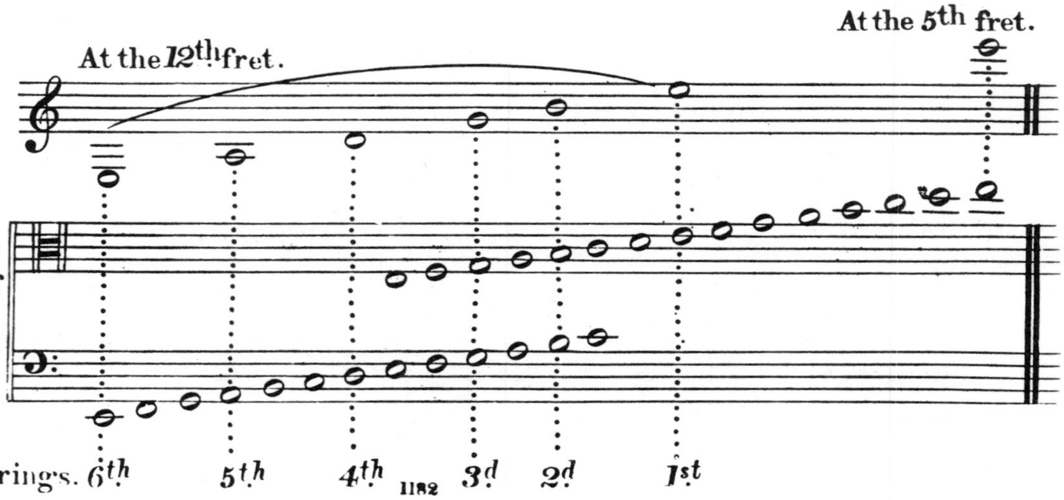

Ex: 78.

Result to be produced

Operation in Harmonics.

Ex: 79.

DUO, *In the Opera of Mozart's "Don Juan".*

Ex: 80.
Voice.
Là ci da-rem la ma..........no, la mi di--rai di
Piano.
Guitar.
si, ve-di non e lon---ta-no, par-tiam ben mi---o da qui. etc:

AIR.

by Paesiello.

Ex: 81.

Nel cor piu non mi sen..to bril..lar la gio..ven.tù, cag..
gion del mio tor....men......to a.....ni..ma mi..a sei tu, mi
pun..gi..chi mi ma.sti..chi, mi piz....zi..chi, mi stuzzichi, che
cos' è questa, ohi mè, pie.....tà, pie...tà, pie.....tà, a...
mo..re è un cer.....to che che de....li....rar mi fà.

PART OF A ROMANCE BY CHERUBINI.

Ex. 82.

Bon Français, Dieu te re.......com...pen.......se, un bien...
fait n'est ja-mais perdu, bon Français, Dieu te re...com..pen...se, un bien..
fait n'est jamais per....du, un bien.fait n'est ja...mais per
...du, n'est jamais per du, n'est jamais per...du.

Ariette by F. Sor.

Ex 83.

Larghetto.
La grime mie d'affan.........no, sos..pi..ri del mio cor, all'
I...dol mio ti...ran...no spie....ga..te il mi o do...lor,
ma, che mi gio...va il pian...to, che gio....va sos..........pi...rar.........
se la crudel in.....tan...........to ri...de del mio pe.........nar,
se la crudel in..tan.....to ri.............de del mi..o pe....nar.

XXVIII

Portion of the first part of Haydn's oratorio, "The Creation"

(See Clementi's Edition of the Creation, Page 6.)

Ex. 84.

del..la not..te le te...nebre or...ren..de
già dis
gombra la splen.........di...da luce del....la
not....te le te..nebre or..ren.......de tut..to il monde gio...is...ce del
dè, tut..to il monde gio..is...ce del dè.
Mai piu mai più mai più con.....fu.....sio.........ne mai
più con....fu...sio....ne non v'e, mai più mai più

mai più mai più mai più confu...sio.....ne non
v'è, mai più con fu..sio..ne non v'e.
L'empio
Stuol di De...mo....ni op..pres.......so
giu nel re.........gno giu nel

re........gno dell' om........bre piom...bò
giu nel re........gno dell'
om........bre piom...bò nel
re........gno dell' om........bre
giu nel re........gno dell'

XXXII

Gabriel. Soprano.
Ariel. Alto.
Raphael. Tenore.
Basso.
Om...bre piom...bò pre....ci..pi...tar
pre.....ci....pi.....tar l'or..go..glio degl' empy il
pre.....ci....pi...tar l'or..go..glio
pre.....ci...pi.....tar pre..ci....pi.......tar l'or
l'or...go..glio degl' empy il ciel mi..rò, degl' empy il ciel mi..
ciel mi.....rò il ciel mi....rò pre..

degl' empy il ciel mi_rò, degl' empy il ciel....... mi.......
go_glio degl' empy il ciel mi.......rò il ciel mi.......
ro pre...ci....pi.....tar l'or go_glio, degl' empy il ciel... mi...
ci....pi.....tar....... l'or go_glio, degl' empy il ciel mi...
rò l'or.....go_glio l'or..
rò pre.....ci.....pi.....tar l'or.....go....glio del
rò pre.........ci.....pi.....tar l'or...
rò pre....ci....pi.........tar l'or_go_glio

em..py degl' em.py il ciel mi......rò .
go..glio degl' em.py il ciel mi......rò .
go.......glio degl' em.py il ciel mi.......rò .
degl' em.py il ciel mi......rò .
1 3 2 1 1 0 2
1
1 3 1 0 3 1
2 1 3 1 3 1 2 1
Del nu..me e..ter..no il so.....glio, del nu.me e..ter.no il
Del nu..me e...ter..no il so.....glio, del nu.me e..ter.no il
Del nu.me e...ter..no il so....glio, del nu.me e..ter.no il
Del nu.me e...ter..no il so....glio, del nu.me e..ter.no il
4 2 4 2 4 2 1 4
1 1 1 4
4

so.....glio più lie........to più lie...........to al...lor res....tò
so.....glio piu lie........to più lie.............to al...lor res......tò
so.....glio più lie........to più lie......to al.........lor res.... tò
so.....glio più lie........to più lie......to al.......lor res......tò
del nume e....ter..no il so.......glio, del nume e..terno il
del nume e....ter..no il so.......glio, del nume e..terno il
del nume e....ter..no il so.......glio, del nume e..terno il
del nume e....ter..no il so.......glio, del nume e..terno il

so glio, più lie.........to più lie............to al...lor res...
so glio, piu lie.........to più lie........to al........lor res........
so glio, piu lie.........to più lie....to al.......lor res........
so glio, più lie.........to più lie.......to al.........lor res........
to
tò.
to. L'empi o stuol lempio stuol di de..mo..ny ap...pres......so
tò.

l'or..
pre..
giu nel re...gno dell' ombre piombò nell' om.....bre piom...
go...glio si l'or....go...glio degl' em.py il ciel mi..
ci....pi....tar l'or...go...glio degl' em....py degl' em.py il ciel mi..
bò pre.....ci.....pi....tar l'or.....go......glio degl' em.py il ciel mi...
pre....ci.....pi....tar l'or....go...glio degl' em.py il ciel mi..

rò,
del nu...me e...ter..no il
rò,
del nu...me e...ter..no il
rò,
del nu...me e...ter...no il
rò,
del nu...me e...ter..no il
so.......glio, del nume e...ter..no il so......glio più lie..........to più
so.......glio, del nume e.....ter..no il so......glio più lie..........to più
so......glio, del nume e...ter..no il so......glio più lie..........to più
so......glio, del nume e...ter..no il so......glio più lie..........to più

lie............to al...lor res......tò . Del
lie.........to al.........lor res..........tò Del
lie............to al....lor res..........tò . Del
lie............to al...lor res..........tò . Del
nume e..terno il so......glio del nume e.....terno il so.....glio più
nume e..terno il so......glio del nume e.....terno il so.....glio più
nume e..terno il so......glio del nume e.....terno il so.....glio più
nume e..terno il so......glio del nume e.....terno il so......glio più

lie.....to più lie...........to al...lor res..tò, più lieto al..lor res..
lie.....to più lie.........to al...lor res..tò, più lieto al..lor res..
lie.....to più lie...........to al...lor res.........tò, più lieto al..lor res..
lie.....to più lie...........to al....lor res.........tò, più lieto al..lor res..
tò, più lie..to al....lor res.....tò.
tò, più lie..to al....lor res.....tò.
tò, più lie..to al....lor res....tò.
tò, più lie..to al....lor res....tò.

Andante.

Ex: 85.

Andante.

Ex: 86.

Ex: 87.

XLII

Fine.

THE LIBRARY
ST. MARY'S COLLEGE OF MARYLAND
ST. MARY'S CITY, MARYLAND 20686

066712